ALSO BY LINDA DONN

Freud and Jung: Years of Friendship, Years of Loss

THE
ROOSEVELT
COUSINS

ALFRED A. KNOPF   NEW YORK

2001

THE
ROOSEVELT
COUSINS

Growing Up Together, 1882-1924

LINDA DONN

THIS IS A BORZOI BOOK
PUBLISHED BY ALFRED A. KNOPF

www.aaknopf.com

Library of Congress Cataloging-in-Publication Data

Donn, Linda.
   The Roosevelt cousins : Growing up together, 1882–1924 / Linda Donn. — 1st ed.
      p.   cm.
   ISBN 0-679-44637-0 (alk. paper)
   1. Roosevelt family. 2. Roosevelt, Theodore, 1858–1919—Family. 3. Longworth, Alice Roosevelt, 1884–1980. 4. Roosevelt, Theodore, 1887–1944. 5. Roosevelt, Franklin D. (Franklin Delano), 1882–1945. 6. Roosevelt, Eleanor, 1884–1962.
   7. Cousins—United States—Biography. I. Title.
   E757.3 .D66 2001
   973.91'092'2—dc21
   [B]
                                                              2001033893

Manufactured in the United States of America

FIRST EDITION

FOR

TONY, CASSIE, ALEX, AND MICHAEL

WITH LOVE

When I was just out of college, I was taken by my father to see *Hamlet* for the first time. At the end I turned to him, dazzled, only to realize that he was not impressed by Richard Burton's portrayal of the tortured Dane.

"That might be *your* idea of Hamlet," my father said, "but it's not mine."

I did not know then that the sexy young prince on the stage was partly the actor's interpretation, and it was some time before I understood that historical figures were vulnerable not only to an actor's vision, or a playwright's, but also to the distortions of time and the constraints of biography. The knowledge took on added significance partway through my research on a generation of Roosevelt cousins—among them Eleanor, Franklin, Alice, and Ted Jr.

At first their story seemed straightforward: I was interested in exploring the echoing images that are the legacies of a close family, and the ties among the cousins were many. They shared similar hopes and fears, were encouraged and comforted by the same relatives, and grew into their political lives together. In the course of my work, among their letters and photographs, I found the ineffable patterns reflective of an affectionate family.

But I also found, as I laid the cousins' lives side by side, that sometimes one person's perceptions belied another's; emotions were likely to distort their impressions, and self-appraisals in diaries and autobiographies occasionally conflicted with the estimations of others. The cousins also contradicted themselves from time to time, writing one thing in a letter, then changing their minds days later in another. They were apt to be unclear. It was not unusual for their actions to be at odds with their interior lives, and a few constructed facades that were taken to be their "real" selves.

Their behavior was normal, of course. Like the rest of us, the cousins were simply living their lives. But the prism of their different perspectives offered fascinating, multiple views of "reality," and rather than try to make them fit together, I decided to convey, at moments, the sense of various realities refracting side by side. I hoped this would present a rich and ultimately truer picture of the Roosevelt family. Recalling Richard Burton's long-ago interpretation of Hamlet, I understood my father's unease, for now I too felt the actor had gripped the character too firmly.

Since I didn't want to try to exert that kind of control, I investigated the anomalies: The chronic inconsistencies of a particular cousin served as a reminder that personality is often fluid; discrepancies among the cousins' accounts revealed aspects of their characters that congruence could not. Sometimes a glancing comment by one shed light on another.

Surprisingly, clarity slowly emerged. At first, it had saddened me to see the cousins' parallel lives ultimately collide, defying the logic of geometry, but not of family life. But increasingly, as I came to know the cousins' separate, necessary struggles, I realized that a person best honors his family by first honoring his conscience. For only in this way can a family remain vital and flexible and, like the Roosevelt clan, capable of casting itself along new lines.

Linda Donn
New York City
March 2001

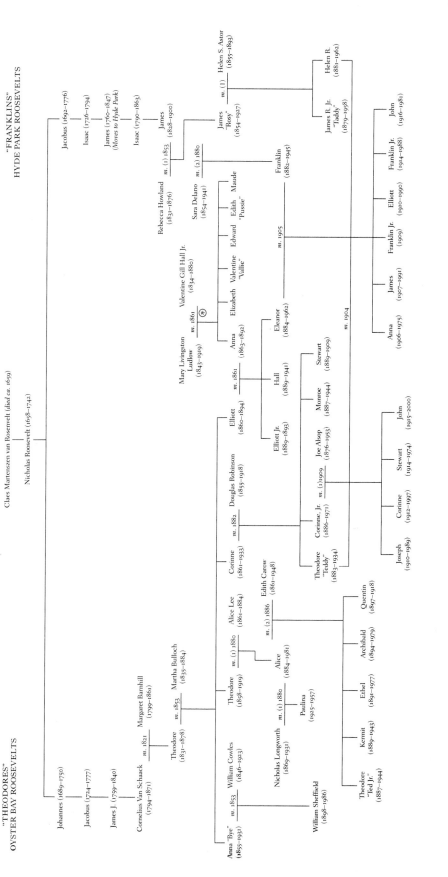

"THEODORES"
OYSTER BAY ROOSEVELTS

"FRANKLINS"
HYDE PARK ROOSEVELTS

Claes Martenszen van Rosenvelt (*died ca.* 1659)

Nicholas Roosevelt (1658–1742)

Johannes (1689–1750)

Jacobus (1724–1777)

James J. (1759–1840)

Jacobus (1692–1776)

Isaac (1726–1794)

James (1760–1847)
(*Moves to Hyde Park*)

Isaac (1790–1863)

James (1828–1900)

Helen S. Astor (1855–1893)

Cornelius Van Schaack (1794–1871)

Margaret Barnhill (1799–1861)

m. 1821

Theodore (1831–1878)

Martha Bulloch (1835–1884)

m. 1853

Rebecca Howland (1831–1876)

m. (1) 1853

James "Rosy" (1854–1927)

Sara Delano (1854–1941)

m. (2) 1880

Helen R. (1881–1962)

James R. Jr. "Taddy" (1879–1958)

Franklin (1882–1945)

Mary Livingston Ludlow (1843–1919)

Valentine Gill Hall Jr. (1834–1880)

m. 1861 ✱

Anna (1863–1892)

Elizabeth

Valentine "Vallie"

Edward

Edith "Pussie"

Maude

Eleanor (1884–1962)

m. 1905

Anna (1906–1975)

James (1907–1991)

Franklin Jr. (1909)

Elliott (1910–1990)

Franklin Jr. (1914–1988)

John (1916–1981)

Elliott (1860–1894)

Hall (1889–1941)

Elliott Jr. (1889–1893)

Stewart (1888–1909)

Monroe (1887–1944)

Anna "Bye" (1855–1931)

William Cowles (1846–1923)

m. 1853

Theodore (1858–1919)

Alice Lee (1861–1884)

m. (1) 1880

Edith Carow (1861–1948)

m. (2) 1886

Corinne (1861–1933)

Douglas Robinson (1855–1918)

m. 1882

Theodore "Teddy" (1883–1934)

Corinne, Jr. (1886–1971)

Joe Alsop (1876–1953)

m. (1) 1909

Joseph (1910–1989)

Corinne (1912–1997)

Stewart (1914–1974)

John (1915–2000)

William Sheffield (1848–1986)

Nicholas Longworth (1869–1931)

m. (1) 1880

Alice (1884–1981)

Paulina (1925–1957)

Theodore "Ted Jr." (1887–1944)

Kermit (1889–1943)

Ethel (1891–1977)

Archibald (1894–1979)

Quentin (1897–1918)

m. 1904

THE
ROOSEVELT
COUSINS

Prologue

December 1902

One morning in December 1902, eighteen-year-old Alice Roosevelt slipped out of the White House into the first snowfall of the year. Wagons floated soundlessly down Pennsylvania Avenue as dark-clad figures stepped high to clear the drifts. President Theodore Roosevelt's daughter and her maid swung into a waiting carriage and joined the silent parade.

Alice knew it was cold inside the buildings she passed on her way to the Baltimore and Potomac train terminal. Although her father had settled the nationwide coal strike two months before, there was still not enough fuel to heat the city. The Houses of Congress had resorted to burning wood in a futile attempt to warm their chambers. Ordinarily Alice would have enjoyed the spectacle of lawmakers conducting business in their overcoats and mufflers. On another day she would have stopped to watch, amused. But now she continued past the Capitol Building, anxious to catch the ten o'clock train to New York, for she planned to have tea that afternoon with her cousin Eleanor Roosevelt.

When she arrived at the entrance to the terminal at Sixth and B Streets, out of habit, Alice raised her chin defensively. The press shadowed the president's daughter everywhere, eager to report the smallest detail of her life to a nation fascinated by "Princess Alice." Theodore Roosevelt had been sworn into office only the year before, when William McKinley was assassinated, and people hadn't tired of reading about Alice—in a yellow dress, her "feathers flying" as she ran up to a crowd of admirers, or, wrapped in lap robes, giggling with a friend in an open carriage.

In the parlor car that morning, inevitably, the passengers glanced curiously at the president's pretty daughter. They had read the articles, and they had heard the rumors—that she bet at the horse races and drove the new automobiles much too fast. But only Alice's friends and family knew the extent of her excesses. How she burst into rooms in gales of laughter ("madly gay," a relative said disapprovingly), unsnapping her pocketbook to let her green pet snake slither out. How she smoked a corncob pipe and courted caffeine highs with quick cups of strong tea, flirting with every boy in sight and talking about the "second establishment" a member of the Astor family kept for his mistress. Theodore Roosevelt worried about his eldest daughter and her endless antics. When a family member told Alice she was born to make herself conspicuous, the eighteen-year-old threatened, "Wait until I am 21!"

The train, its flower vases bolted to the walls, rattled up the coast through falling snow as waiters served Champagne, considered an antidote to travel sickness. Six hours later, Alice arrived in New York City in the yellow dusk of engine lights and coal smoke. Traffic was snarled in the streets, and it was nearly dark when she and her maid finally drew up to the brownstone at 11 West 37th Street, where Eleanor Roosevelt lived.

Orphaned as a child, eighteen-year-old Eleanor lived with relatives who were becoming increasingly unstable. That December, Mary Hall, her grandmother, was trying to sequester Eleanor's alcoholic uncle Vallie in the country, but sometimes he escaped and returned to the brownstone, where his drunken tirades humiliated Eleanor. Worse, once or twice Vallie had arrived brandishing a pistol. Eleanor's chaperone, thirty-two-year-old Aunt Pussie, was no help. Volatile herself and self-absorbed, Pussie flew into rages over her failed love affairs and shut herself in her room for days at a

Eleanor Roosevelt, daughter of
Elliott Roosevelt, as a young woman
in New York

Alice Roosevelt, daughter of
President Theodore Roosevelt

time, refusing to talk or eat. Eleanor later wrote that only those who knew the "entire situation" were invited to dine or spend the night at their country house, and things were no better in the city.

Alice and Eleanor were the same age, the eldest children of two brothers, Theodore and Elliott Roosevelt; both their mothers had long been dead. But aside from these superficial similarities, out of some twenty-five Roosevelt cousins born in the 1880s, the two girls seemed the most unalike. That winter, two techniques were thought fashionable for managing long skirts in the snow. Alice probably pulled hers taut against her body to outline the curve of her hip as she walked up the steps of the house. Eleanor didn't play at the edge of propriety the way her cousin did; if she greeted Alice outside, no doubt she looped her skirt in front of her modestly.

Eleanor later wrote that she lacked confidence as a teenager and was "a little afraid" of Alice, who seemed "much older and cleverer." In the years to come, when "poor Eleanor" became the object of Alice's relentless derision, people assumed they had never been friends, and biographers made little reference to any closeness between them.

But on December 5, 1902, although Alice would eventually see many of her cousins on her trip to New York, she traveled through a blizzard to visit Eleanor first.

FOUR DAYS LATER, on December 9, twenty-year-old Franklin Roosevelt left his home on the Hudson River in Hyde Park and arrived in New York City in time for lunch with his distant cousin Eleanor. Reacquainted when she returned from England after several years in boarding school, they had spent an evening in November at the Madison Square Garden Horse Show, and they would have tea together once or twice that December. Eleanor was self-deprecating by nature, and people who later read her autobiography would wonder why good-looking Franklin had taken an interest in a homely girl with few friends and little to offer in the way of either amusing banter or serious conversation.

After lunch, Eleanor and Franklin joined the throngs of Christmas shoppers. Monogramming was popular that season, and women ordered their husbands' initials engraved on the silver handles of umbrellas and sewn on the silk cuffs of dressing gowns. The economy was so strong that diamond rings instead of the usual good-luck coins had been baked in some of the English plum puddings crossing the Atlantic, but charity workers on the street corners still shook handbells and collected money from passersby. The Salvation Army needed to fill 22,500 baskets with food by Christmas morning and serve three thousand hot turkey dinners at tables laid end to end down the huge exhibition hall above Grand Central train terminal at Park Avenue and Forty-third Street. It was a family tradition for Roosevelt cousins to serve at such holiday meals. Eleanor and Alice's grandfather Theodore Roosevelt Sr.—called "Greatheart" for his generosity—had worked at the family importing and banking house during the day, but many of his evenings had been spent at the shelter he established for homeless boys. His sons, Theodore and Elliott, had set a similar example for their children, and on Christmas Day Eleanor planned to give out candy at the Newsboys' Lodging House.

The weeks before Christmas marked the height of New York's social season, and on December 9, after their lunch and shopping excursion, Eleanor and Franklin joined Alice at a dance given for their cousin Christine Kean at Sherry's, a fashionable Fifth Avenue restaurant. Other cousins joined them, and Alice and Eleanor, assigning the seating for the party the night before, had arranged for a young Roosevelt to preside at each of the six tables. Eleanor was one of the hostesses, but it was not a position she enjoyed. She wrote later that boys rarely asked her to dance at parties, and recalled her "gratitude" when Franklin asked her once, just to be nice.

The united front of cousins at Christine's dance would not have surprised young Nicholas Roosevelt. When he and his cousins lined up for photographs, the frieze of young Roosevelts showed him that his family

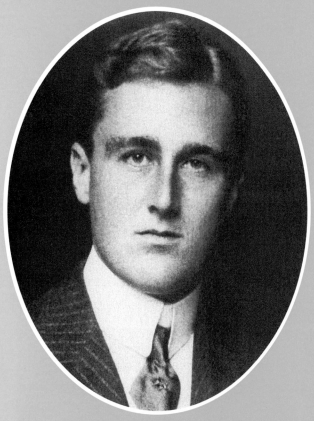

*Portrait of Theodore Roosevelt Sr.,
father of Anna (Bye), Theodore,
Elliott, and Corinne*

*Franklin Delano Roosevelt, son of James Roosevelt,
at the turn of the twentieth century*

A typical frieze of Roosevelt cousins

"personified" loyalty. He knew the Roosevelts "embraced forebears, living and dead, as well as cousins to the fifth degree."

Franklin was a "fifth degree" cousin, and as he came through the receiving line, one Roosevelt or another quite likely thought the elegant young man might want to marry Alice. A newspaper reported that she looked pretty in pink tulle, holding a matching bouquet of pink roses as she stood next to Christine and greeted the guests. But years later, when asked in interviews about her Hyde Park cousin, Alice claimed that he had been nothing more than "a good little mother's boy" and remembered calling him "Feather Duster" (after the initials for Franklin Delano) because he "pranced around and fluttered." She bragged that her Oyster Bay family had rowed "sweatingly" while his had only sailed.

Whatever the internal dynamics among the three cousins in December 1902, their strengths seemed indistinct—as indistinguishable from those of the other cousins as their faces in childhood photographs. Alice, Eleanor, and Franklin gave no indication of being better equipped than the rest to play pivotal roles in American history. There was no sign that these three cousins would create an unparalleled political epic.

However, several sources taken together—among them diaries Alice kept as a young woman, an obscure little book Eleanor wrote at the end of her life, and archival interviews—contribute to a more complete picture of the three young Roosevelts. The papers shed light on the true characters of these complex people and the actual relationships among them. Contrary to the descriptions Eleanor gives in her memoir of having been awkward and unsure, a friend remembered her, even at eighteen, as "a noble person." And Eleanor herself, in a book written late in her life, reveals that from the first she had been relaxed and talkative with Franklin, whom she describes as intellectually curious and ambitious. Alice writes in her diary of her admiration for Eleanor, and confesses her own lack of confidence in entry after entry. Far from secure, Alice seems to have sought her cousin's company for reassurance and support.

This closeness among the three cousins adds an affecting dimension as family tradition draws them into political life and into competition with one another. Jealousies and betrayals contribute to their estrangement when Franklin's dramatic political ascent signals as steep a fall for Alice's brother Ted. By 1924, resentments within the family have silenced friendships born in baby carriages.

The story begins in 1884 with twenty-five-year-old Theodore Roosevelt, the future president, who would be a forceful presence in the cousins' lives for thirty-five years. That February his daughter Alice had just been born, and he faced an ordeal that threatened to destroy him.

PART ONE

YOUNG COUSINS

1882–1902

Theodore

ON FEBRUARY 16, 1884, at a little before ten in the morning, horses walked side by side down Fifth Avenue pulling two hearses. They carried matching rosewood coffins covered with wreaths of white roses and lilies. Theodore's mother, Martha, had succumbed to typhoid fever on February 14; eleven hours later his young wife died after having given birth to their daughter.

Nothing had prepared the young state assemblyman for what had been given and taken away in the same furious instant. Theodore's face was expressionless at the funeral. His older sister, Anna, whom everyone called Bye, led him about like a small, unfocused child. Later, in the family house at 6 West 57th Street, as she listened to the rhythmic tread of his boots on the floor above, Bye worried that her brother was losing his mind. The next day Theodore held his infant daughter in his arms, a locket of her mother's yellow hair around her neck, and christened her Alice, after his dead wife.

Alice Hathaway Lee had grown up with four sisters and a brother in Chestnut Hill, Massachusetts, next door to five first cousins, the children of the Leverett Saltonstall family. Eleven boys and girls had spent their childhood running back and forth across the lawn that joined the two clapboard houses, sure of being home wherever they went. Later, when one of the Saltonstall cousins, Richard, invited his Harvard friends home to Chestnut Hill, bespectacled and energetic Theodore was struck by Alice Lee. Her blue eyes were pale, and at the same time bright, as if an artist had sharpened them with a touch of white paint.

Theodore had had a secret understanding with his childhood love, Edith Carow, but they had quarreled, and he began courting Alice Lee in his junior year at Harvard. When his extravagant nature and impetuous pursuit frightened her away, he was shaken by her withdrawal and walked all night in the woods around Cambridge. Friends, alarmed, sent a telegram to his family in New York, and a Roosevelt cousin, a medical student, was dispatched to find Theodore and calm him down. It was rumored that when Alice rebuffed him again, in Bar Harbor, Maine, he attempted suicide. At another low point, Theodore ordered a set of French dueling pistols. "I did not think I could win her and I went nearly crazy at the mere thought of losing her," he confessed.

But in the end Theodore prevailed, and they were married in October 1880. "They are both so well and bright that they are like sunbeams, everyone loving them," Theodore's aunt Annie Gracie said of the young couple six months before Alice Lee died.

After the funerals, Theodore returned to Albany and threw himself back into his state-assembly work. He kept up a feverish pace and barely slept, but when the session ended, he chose not to seek reelection. His political career, he told Bye, now mattered little to him. The year before, he had become a partner in a cattle business, and he decided to move out West to his ranch in the Dakotas, leaving young Alice with Bye.

The inhospitable terrain of the Badlands—like "Hell with the fires out," one observer wrote—suited Theodore. Two thousand miles from his baby, with his wife and his mother dead, he courted every challenge and grew gaunt—"thin-flanked," one newspaper reported. A friend said, "You could have spanned his waist with your two thumbs and fingers." Theodore bankrupted his body and didn't care. He was finishing work he had begun as a child.

Theodore's mother,
Martha Bulloch Roosevelt

Alice Hathaway Lee,
Theodore Roosevelt, and her first cousin
Rose Saltonstall in 1879

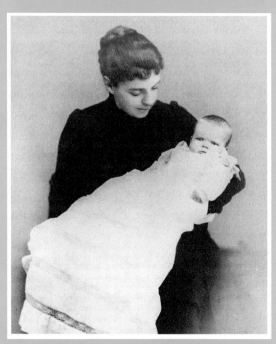

Baby Alice, held by her aunt Bye,
Theodore's older sister

Theodore at the age of eight

Theodore's cabin in the Badlands of North Dakota

Asthma had plagued Theodore when he was a boy, and he had been clumsy and not athletic; he had lived, he later wrote, "much at home." But he had undergone a transformation when, as a fourteen-year-old, he took up bodybuilding and learned to box. He took to the sport slowly; "sheer industry" had seen him through. The boy had also struggled to be brave, inspired by the story of the British sea captain Frederick Marryat, who became courageous, as Theodore put it, "by sheer dint of practicing fearlessness." Sometimes Theodore called it willpower; at other times he called it deliberate determination. But at an early age he developed an existential belief in the need to create himself. "By acting as if I was not afraid," he later wrote, "I gradually ceased to be afraid." It was a lesson his niece Eleanor would also learn at a young age.

Out West, Theodore rarely spoke of the depression that haunted him, but his business partner William Sewall remembered his saying once that he "didn't have anything to live for. He was as blue a man as you ever see. I went right for him bow-legged. I told him he had no right to talk that way. He had his child to bring up. He said Alice would never know."

"Her aunt can take care of her a good deal better than I can," Theodore told his business partner. "She would be just as well off without me." The young widower seemed "used up" in the spring of 1885, "all teeth and eyes," as one observer put it, and the Roosevelts were so worried that they asked Sewall to look after him. "They had no business to write to you, they should have written to me," Theodore said.

"I guess they knew you wouldn't write about how you were getting on," his partner replied. "You'd just say you were all right."

One cold day in April, the Little Missouri River was a fast-running tide of mountain water and ice floes. John Fisher was cutting and hauling ice on the riverbank when Theodore rode up on his horse Manitou and asked where the dam was. Fisher was surprised. "You surely won't try to cross on the dam when you can go and cross on the trestle the way the others do?" The water was coursing so high that the dam couldn't be seen. "It's more than likely that there's not much of the dam left," Fisher warned.

"It doesn't matter," Theodore said. "Manitou's a good swimmer and we're going across."

But the dam had crumbled partway across the flooding river. Manitou lost his footing, and Fisher knew that if the horse drifted even a little downstream, he and his rider would never get ashore. But Theodore kept shoving chunks of ice away from his horse's head, and Manitou held his own against the current for the quarter of a mile across the Little Missouri. They were safe. The reckless ride showed John Fisher that Theodore could survive almost anything. In 1912, when Fisher heard that his friend had been shot, he didn't worry about "the man who could swim the Little Missouri on horseback when it was running bank full and blocks of ice as big as a house."

Soaking wet, Theodore rode up to the general store on the far bank. In the years to come, the shopkeeper, Joe Ferris, would also tell the story of the time Theodore and Manitou had crossed the river, and he'd always end by saying *he* "wouldn't have taken that swim for all of Dakota." That afternoon in Ferris's store, Theodore bought a pair of dry socks and put them on. The Little Missouri had decided that he should live.

Within weeks of his river crossing, Theodore headed East. Before he went, he turned his saddle horses out on the range and left word that no one was ever to ride them or sell them. From time to time the cowboys caught sight of some of the horses, but never Manitou. One by one over the years the horses died on the range, and in the summers when the snows melted, the cowboys would come upon their bodies. But no one ever found a trace of Manitou.

Alice and Eleanor

THEODORE WAS EXPECTED HOME from the West early in the summer of 1885. Shortly before his arrival, Edith Carow came to spend a week with one of his aunts in Oyster Bay, a semi-wilderness of water and chestnut woods on the north shore of Long Island, thirty miles east of New York City. Theodore and his brother and sisters had grown up in New York with Edith. Their nurses had pushed them across Union Square in their carriages. As they got older, the friendship between Edith and Theodore became especially close, and when the Roosevelt family sailed to Europe for a year, she kept the letters she received from him, together with a curl of his hair, locked up in a little box.

Everyone was surprised when they did not marry. Years later, Theodore told his sister Bye that in 1878, when Edith was seventeen and he was twenty, they had "very intimate relations," but that there "came a break." Edith maintained that Theodore had not been nice, though a story she wrote when she was fifteen suggests her own youthful conflicts. The heroine found the hero, "Rex," the epitome of all human excellence, and he in turn had "lost his whole loving heart" to her. But the girl dreaded Rex's great love and was afraid to let him come too close. Once when they were

Alice and Ted with Edith Roosevelt, holding Kermit

Theodore as a Harvard student in 1878

Sagamore Hill, gathering place for the Roosevelt cousins

out walking together, a burr pricked her finger and Rex—"poor foolish Rex"—took her wounded hand in his larger, warmer one and kissed it.

"How dare you," the girl cried, and, in her "dusky brown dress with a bit of red at the throat," ran from him like a "hunted deer."

Theodore had taken care not to see Edith on his visits East after Alice Lee's death—not even a glimpse in the drawing rooms of relatives and friends. Victorian propriety dictated that a gentleman should not marry a second time. To do so would put a lie to his first love. Theodore's torment was that he agreed with his fellow Victorians, but he was also young, with a tumultuous and ardent nature. Now more than a year had passed since his wife had died, and only a bit of woods would lie between him and Edith. But she, learning of Theodore's impending arrival, quickly decamped to New Jersey, and it wasn't until a few months later that they accidentally encountered each other in Bye's house.

Theodore had changed considerably since Edith had seen him last. No longer the boy she had known, he had gained an astonishing thirty pounds since his river crossing, and there were subtler changes, too. Theodore had always had a sense of the fragility of life and a familiarity with suffering, but now they had risen to the surface and were shadowing his face. Edith would not turn from that.

They married in December 1886 and moved to his new house in Oyster Bay the following summer, bringing Alice, who was nearly three and a half. Theodore had designed Sagamore Hill from the inside out, paying more attention to the use and flow of the rooms than to the aesthetics of the structure itself. He made sure that the huge fireplaces took the logs he liked to chop and that his study companionably flanked Edith's parlor, but the outside had an ungainly air. Four boys and a girl (in order, Ted, Kermit, Ethel, Archibald, and Quentin) were born between 1887 and 1897, and Sagamore Hill became the family's favorite place.

Theodore wrote Bye that he found Alice "too good and happy for anything." He told his younger sister, Corinne Robinson, that he missed his daughter when she did not come and sit in her chair in her long white nightgown to watch him shave. But the little girl was also a constant reminder and rebuke. Theodore had loved his first wife passionately; he had driven her memory before him in wild rides across the West. Young Alice personified his grief, so vividly did she resemble the beautiful girl who had been his wife. And because Theodore believed he had betrayed Alice Lee by remarrying, his daughter bore the brunt of what she would describe as his "guilt fetish."

Even as a young girl, Alice was an arresting figure with a commanding presence, but at times she clung pathetically to her nurse, Jane. Her aunts worried that she did not seem "to relish either meat or vegetables," and Edith noticed that she could look pale and sickly, like a "quiet and mousy person." Theodore did not recognize this vulnerability in his daughter. He teasingly called her "stony hearted." He tried in vain once, when she was going to visit her grandparents in Boston, to elicit some sign that she did not want to leave him. Dressed in her best, looking just like a "little white penguin," his daughter had not cried; he had left her too many times for that. But Alice was not without feeling. "Saying good-bye to Father was a choky, though tearless business," she confessed years later. "I always felt a little gulpy when I said good-bye to him; for any length of time—not only when I was a child."

ELEANOR WAS BORN eight months after her cousin Alice. Theodore's younger brother, twenty-four-year-old Elliott, had married Anna Hall, a beautiful girl from the Hudson River Valley; she gave birth to their daughter on October 11, 1884.

Like Theodore, Elliott had been gravely shaken when their mother died, and the family hoped his young wife would be a comfort to him. But Anna's haunting beauty hid a troubled nature. Her childhood had been dominated by an eccentric and religious father who placed great importance on self-discipline. Valentine Hall made his daughter take walks several times a day with a stick laid across her back, the ends held firmly in the crook of her elbows. Anna was slender and pale because she was often

Alice, age four

Eleanor's mother,
Anna Hall Roosevelt

Roosevelt children bathing at Oyster Bay

unwell, but her distinctive carriage was eloquent testimony to her father's control. She grew up the child most like him, as serious and high-minded.

But when he died, Anna tried to cast off his legacies: the tyranny of self-denial and the constant, austere dialogue with God. At nineteen she welcomed marriage to Elliott Roosevelt, and it seemed a good match at first. Anna had a flawless social presence—she was said to be tuned to a ballroom pitch—and he was a handsome, pleasure-seeking young man with a taste for fashionable society. But soon Anna began to return to her childhood home, sometimes for six months at a time. And she took her daughter, Eleanor, with her, up the driveway through small steel gates, past the stone gatehouse and stables and the lawn shaded by towering oaks, to the large stuccoed house.

Oak Terrace, in the village of Tivoli, was one of many estates fortressed by the headlands that rose above the Hudson River. Residents called the freedom that came from the steep terrain living in "the shadow of the mountains." The enclave was linked by a private road that had been cleared through the woods along the river. For most people, the freedom to do as they wished unfolded gently eccentric lives.

But for others it meant unlicensed opportunity. Eight young Astor children had the run of the nearby Rokeby estate after the deaths of their mother and father. The orphans' vast fortune was administered by trustees, and their wishes were catered to by a staff of governesses, tutors, nurses, cooks, seamstresses, butlers, grooms, and gardeners, but no one seemed to be in charge. The orphans brought themselves up, child by child, devising rules and rituals that were a bizarre mix of sensitivity and cruelty, and a consequence of living out of public view.

Eleanor's relatives were as eccentric. Alcoholism afflicted the males in the family, and she grew up surrounded by careless men. Late at night, the bartender in the local tavern would load Eleanor's uncles Vallie and Eddie Hall into their carriage, the horse finding his way back to Oak Terrace while they slept. In the daytime, young cousins made a game of creeping Indian-file through the fields, closer and closer to the lawn at

Oak Terrace, and waited to see who would be the first to run if Vallie shot at them from an upstairs window. A generation later one of Eleanor's sons remembered being frightened every time he visited the mansion on the river.

Elliott Roosevelt had been a gentle and uncertain boy who sometimes wrote of himself as a girl, but he had grown into a dashing young man determined to be a good husband. That hope ended when his mother died, for he lost his bearings, and it became apparent that he was an alcoholic. Time after time, Elliott promised not to drink, but he was unable to keep his word, and Anna felt increasingly helpless. "I woke up with one of my terrible headaches," she told a friend one day. "I could not move or think." But in spite of the disease that was destroying him, Elliott struggled to give the best of himself to his daughter before the last wave of alcoholism overtook him. "I never doubted," Eleanor wrote, "that I stood first in his heart."

Elliott's condition had deteriorated badly by the spring of 1887, when Eleanor was two and a half years old. The Roosevelt family decided that a few months' treatment abroad was his only hope. On May 18, Elliott, Anna, and Eleanor set sail on the *Britannic*. On the second day out, passengers on the upper deck saw the iron prow of a steamer loom out of the heavy fog. The *Celtic,* off course, rammed into the *Britannic* and broke through its port side. Before the steamer finally cleared the *Britannic's* stern, the ships had collided twice more, crushing at least six passengers on the liner and sweeping others into the sea.

The *Britannic* listed. A few men commandeered a lifeboat, climbing back out of it only when the captain drew his pistol. Pinned beneath wreckage, a young child reached desperately for its mother. Lanterns danced eerily in the fog, and horns and bells pierced the cries of women and children. Eleanor dangled over the side of the ship, clutching the sailor who held her. She would not let him swing her down into the arms of her father, who waited in the lifeboat below. Finally the sailor pried her fingers loose, and Eleanor dropped to safety. The *Britannic* made its way back to New York after a burial at dawn, when five bodies and "one unknown leg"

Elliott Jr., left, and Hall with their father,
Elliott, and sister, Eleanor

The cousins' aunt Annie Gracie,
who often took care of them when
their parents traveled

Young Roosevelts playing on the lawn at Sagamore Hill; in foreground, Alice and Ted Jr.

were lowered over the side. The ship was escorted by two steamers and the *Celtic*. With the hole in her side covered only by mattresses lashed with chains, the *Britannic* would never have withstood a gale.

Anna and Elliott set out for Europe again several days later, but Eleanor stayed behind with her great-aunt Annie Gracie, who often took care of Roosevelt children in her Oyster Bay house when their parents traveled. The Long Island fishing village was something of a Roosevelt compound, for Theodore and two of his first cousins, Emlen and J. West, had built houses for their growing families on adjoining land. Alice and her siblings often played with their cousins Christine, Margaret, and George, Emlen Roosevelt's children; and with J. West's daughter, Lorraine, and four sons, Lewis, Oliver, Nicholas, and Harold. Nicholas later remembered that the cousins led a life so self-contained that few non-Roosevelts took part in their affairs.

Eleanor thrived in Oyster Bay. For six months she found herself in a place where laughter drifted across lawns and verandas were luminous in the thick sea air. In the evenings, as the adults sat outside to catch the breeze from the bay, she and Alice chased fireflies with their cousins until darkness enfolded them and they were called home to bed. Years later, Eleanor described herself as having been a solemn little girl, "even when I danced," but her aunt offered glimpses of a very different, enchanting child. "She has such a gentle, generous, affectionate nature," Annie Gracie wrote, "it is impossible not to love her. She talks incessantly and a great deal of it is about 'Baby Lee' "—the family's name for Alice.

Alice and Eleanor were inseparable during the summer of 1887 and for several summers to come. Nearly every morning, Alice left Sagamore Hill in a pony cart with her maid and drove over to visit her cousin. When the girls were older, Anna would write that her daughter, Eleanor, "won't hear of going home as she says, she would not have Alice any more"; they had their lessons in the morning with Annie Gracie and then, "too funny together," they roamed from cottage to cottage like trusting puppies, over the stile to Bye's house and up the steps of Sagamore Hill. A family member noted how "beautifully" Alice played with Eleanor as they shared sandwiches at picnics and chorused the lines of Theodore's favorite songs. Alice even shared her father, who clasped Eleanor in his arms and burst the buttons on her dress in his love for her.

As soon as Anna and Elliott arrived home in the fall of 1887, it was clear their stay in Europe had not helped him. Alice knew, even at a young age, that something was terribly wrong with Eleanor's father. Her relatives stopped talking about him as soon as she came into the room, and so she took to listening at keyholes. Years later, Nicholas, like his cousin Alice, sensed by their silence "the completeness" of his family's disapproval of wayward members.

When Eleanor returned to her parents, the sight of the girl's empty bed saddened Annie Gracie. "I long for my little Eleanor," she wrote, "who so often lit here like a little storm tost bird and made such sweetness and peace for us."

River Families

"WELCOME BACK TO THE DEAR RIVER," Sara Delano Roosevelt was fond of saying. She thought there was no other, better place to live than in her clapboard house in Hyde Park on the bluff high above the Hudson. The Roosevelt home was not much more than a country farmhouse, but Sara preferred it to the brand-new Vanderbilt mansion nearby or the Hall estate in Tivoli some miles up the river road. It was handsome outside, painted tan with dark brown trim, though visitors found the inside unappealing, crowded with old wicker chairs and bric-a-brac.

Franklin was born there on January 30, 1882, and his parents settled him in the room at the top of a tower that rose above the roofline. He was a happy baby, laughing at holiday parties, but he often struggled to get off his mother's lap to try to dance with the older children. Sara knew early that part of Franklin resisted her. When he was a small child, he shocked her by biting neatly into a water goblet. She managed to get the pieces of glass out of his mouth and settle him back at the lunch table, but he continued to eye her with an "impish glint," she later wrote, pretending to take another bite. He had issued a warning of sorts, that aspects of him were beyond her control.

When Franklin grew older, he refused to wear the Little Lord

Fauntleroy suits and the kilts—he called them skirts—his mother wanted to dress him in, and he insisted that a barber cut his long blond curls. Small boys often while away the time in the kitchen in the hope of treats, but Franklin went there reluctantly with Sara, and he refused to speak with the servants when they joked and gave him cookies.

Franklin was happy outside with his father. Every morning from the time he was a baby, James carried him off to the barn to feed the horses and over the fields to check the crops. His father laughed easily, and Franklin's laugh would be like his. Old men in the village of Hyde Park always spoke of James with affection. He often stopped by the village schoolhouse to sit at a desk in the back and listen to the children recite their lessons, and he helped them weave ropes of greens around their classroom windows at Christmastime. As a vestryman at St. James Church, James passed the plate every week for the offering, and years later Eleanor praised the "homely philosophy" that had made him want to "pool his interests" with those of his poorer neighbors.

James's kindliness was grounded in a humanism that was enlightened for his day. Examples given by Eleanor, Sara, and a few other relatives were collected by Rita Hale Kleeman in *Young Franklin Roosevelt*. According to Kleeman, who also wrote a biography of Sara, *Gracious Lady,* James took care to tell his son about the meetings he had attended during the Civil War to help escaping slaves. And one day, when Franklin asked him why his friends refused to play with the tailor's son, James talked about anti-Semitism—the tailor's boy was Jewish—and about his contempt for it. On another occasion, seeing Franklin and Edmund Rogers fistfighting, James told them about the time he'd watched two Chinese men arguing angrily. He said he had asked another Chinese man why they didn't come to blows. "We all know," the man said, "that the man who strikes first has run out of arguments." Franklin absorbed the compassion inherent in his father's simple stories. As a nine-year-old he accompanied James, in increasingly poor health, to a spa in Germany, where a young patient who was confined to a wheelchair would never forget how "very kind" Franklin had been to him.

Franklin in Hyde Park in 1885

Franklin hated the kilts that his mother,
Sara Delano Roosevelt, made him wear.

Franklin and a playmate learning about sailboats in 1888

James also taught his son about outdoor life—how to identify birds, ride a pony, shoot guns, and handle boats. In winter he and Franklin sailed their iceboat on the Hudson, on ice that rose and fell on four-foot tides that rushed upriver from the Atlantic Ocean and hours later flowed back down. People often raced the trains that ran along the east bank, and as a teenager Franklin took out his own boat, the *Hawk,* whenever he could.

From earliest childhood, Franklin wanted to become a sailor and go to sea, and he never tired of the pirate tales his governess told. His "virile, blood-curdling tastes" dismayed Sara. They were in such contrast to the "little boy I tried futilely to make him." Franklin's cousin Laura Delano remembered that he "resented awfully" the way his mother "tried to run him." Years later, Eleanor agreed. She recalled that in his "fight for independence" from his mother, "Franklin was as determined as she was."

Structuring Franklin's life came as second nature to Sara. Her father had owned clipper ships, and her mother, on a voyage to China, had made sure Sara never missed her daily lessons, her early bedtime, or fresh milk from the cow she had brought on board. Sara thought the order her mother had achieved on a square-rigged schooner should surely be replicated for Franklin on dry land. Even in the summer, when the family visited their cottage on Campobello Island off the Maine coast, her son continued to have his lessons every morning.

History came alive for Franklin in the stories his parents told. He was interested to learn that his great-grandmother had wrapped a black sash around her waist on the day Washington died; that his mother had worn a black armband on Lincoln's assassination, and men and women had wept in the streets. But when James told his son about runaway slaves, Franklin was more than interested. "Oh for freedom," he said suddenly, and told his parents that he felt neither free nor happy, because of his lessons at nine, his swim at noon, and bed at eight.

James, in a discussion with his wife, told her she "nagged" the boy, and together they realized, Sara later wrote, that "unconsciously" they had monitored Franklin too closely. To give their son a sense of autonomy, they told him he could do whatever he wanted the next day. Inevitably,

Franklin's experiment in freedom ended when he came home for dinner. He never asked for that kind of day again, but his plea for independence echoed for the length of his childhood.

GENERATIONS OF ROOSEVELTS had lived in the Hudson River valley, descendants of Claes Martenszen, who had emigrated from the Netherlands. He had added "van Rosenvelt" to his name to indicate the town he came from, and his two grandsons adopted Roosevelt as their name. Franklin was descended from Jacobus, who had settled along the Hudson, while Eleanor and Alice belonged to Johannes's branch in Manhattan and on Long Island.

The Hudson River valley was like a small colonial outpost, far from the bustle of the rest of the world elbowing its way into the twentieth century. Eleanor and Franklin grew up sharing the color and feel of the valley, and their lives moved no faster than a horse's fastest stride. As babies, they were carried in wicker seats on the backs of donkeys, and when they were older, they drove their pony carts along the river road. Each time a carriage was rolled out of the barn, its wheels destroyed a design the groom had made on the floor with stencils and different colors of sand. When the buggy rolled back in and the floor was swept, the man drew the picture again.

These slow repetitions mapped Franklin's childhood like the rings on his father's oak trees, and Sara made sure her son could always call up memories of Hyde Park. Years later, he sat in the White House on the shabby wicker chairs she shipped from home, and he ate his porridge with butter-yellow Hyde Park cream so thick he had to ladle it on.

Eleanor's life at Oak Terrace followed similar customs, although her childhood was less secure. Her brother Elliott Jr. was born in 1889, and while a friend recalled vividly how much Eleanor "adored that baby," her own memory was of feeling unable to please her mother the way her little brother did. Two years later, Anna gave birth to a second boy, Gracie Hall.

Franklin and his father, James, in Hyde Park, 1891

*Eleanor and one of her younger
brothers, Elliott Jr.*

*Looking north up the Hudson River,
flanked by headlands*

"I became very self-conscious, with an inordinate desire for praise and a fear of scoldings," Eleanor later wrote. She believed her mother did not like her because she was plain—the "old-fashioned" child whom beautiful Anna sometimes called "granny."

Eleanor once confessed to a friend that she had "hated [her] mother" because she had been unkind, but in fact their relationship was more complicated. All her life, Anna had become anxious when approval was withheld. A lifelong friend found her "peculiarly sensitive." Anna noticed the subtlest change in a voice or attitude, and she became fearful when she thought she had failed to please. Insecure, Anna passed her anxieties on to Eleanor, who took on her mother's hand-me-down fears as her own.

Although Eleanor has been considered largely blameless in her uneasy relations with her mother, she once made a comment that implied another dimension. She wrote that Anne Frank must have been an "exasperating child." Eleanor found Anne quite normal in some ways, but in others "so sensitive, so thoughtful and so conscious of her own personality that she must have been the most trying child to her elders." Eleanor may have recognized that it was difficult to raise a sensitive child, a child not unlike herself, though she may not have realized that the task was even harder when mother and daughter shared the same anxieties.

Perhaps as a consequence of her tendency to be easily hurt, Eleanor developed an empathy for people in difficulty. When Anna had a headache, it pleased the little girl to rub her mother's forehead. When the family went hiking in Italy, five-year-old Eleanor led her donkey while the boy whose job it was sat in the saddle dangling his bleeding feet. She never forgot the little homeless boys in the New York City lodging house—established by her grandfather Theodore Sr.—she visited as a child. But despite her sensitivity, she was too young to understand the strain that Elliott's alcoholism placed on her mother.

Like many daughters, Eleanor was drawn to her father, and she made it clear where her loyalty lay. Partly this may have been at her mother's expense, for Anna seems to have been genuinely concerned about

Eleanor's well-being. She had her daughter sleep in her room, and she missed her when they were separated. They knelt together in prayer every morning, then breakfasted together. In the late afternoons, Eleanor sat on her mother's lap while Anna read stories aloud, and they played tag and other games. When Eleanor was eight years old, Anna organized a group of little girls to study in the family schoolroom. Worried that she was not a stimulating mother, Anna told a friend that she wanted to study science and French history in order to keep up with Eleanor. "*I must* know all this, for my children's sake at least," Anna said.

Years later, in describing her childhood, Eleanor wrote that she had been afraid of nearly everything. But when she listed her fears in her autobiography, they nonetheless led, like the path in a fairy tale, to the courageous figure she later became. Eleanor's version of her childhood was tacitly the story of Cinderella, in which the requisite wicked stepmother was Grandmother Hall, who was strict and remote. And she wrote about taking care of her vain and selfish aunt Pussie as faithfully as Cinderella had looked after her stepsisters. The godmother in Eleanor's fairy tale was her boarding school headmistress, Marie Souvestre. Thanks to her, Eleanor wrote, she gained confidence. She rose from figurative ashes to marry the prince: Franklin. The fact that Eleanor's Cinderella myth is often repeated bears out the observation that history is agreed-upon fable.

Franklin and Eleanor once argued about the possibility of writing an honest autobiography. Eleanor said she thought she could, but Franklin said he didn't think it was possible. Despite his doubts, he encouraged Eleanor over the years to write honestly and freely. There is a story that when she asked him once if she should change something in a column she was writing, he said, "Lady, it's a free country." But his reaction to her autobiography was a different story. According to one of their sons, Franklin edited Eleanor's memoir "ruthlessly."

The poet Archibald MacLeish was among those who puzzled over how the frightened girl of Eleanor's autobiography became a dauntless woman. He could not find a motivating, transforming thread, and finally he threw up his hands. He resorted to another fairy tale in his little biography of Eleanor and wrote that, like Sleeping Beauty, she had slept until she was "awakened by a touch" and was turned miraculously into a brave and shining figure.

At the end of her life, and long after Franklin had died, Eleanor finally explained in some detail what had motivated her from the time she was a very young child. A moment came, Eleanor wrote, when she had to make a difficult choice. Probably she was not yet five when her father led a pony out of the stable and announced that it was time she learned to ride. Eleanor was frightened, but stronger than her fear was her wish to please her father. She mounted the pony, and discovered that she could do something she was afraid of if she made up her mind to it. She also found that her fear lessened every time she rode. Soon she was "actually enjoying our rides over the country roads."

Slowly, willpower became the touchstone of Eleanor's character. She wrote that she was "still small" when she realized she was able to overcome fear, "not conscious" for some time of the momentous lesson she had taught herself. Eleanor seemed a biddable and passive child, but inside she was all activity. As Theodore had years before, she was laboriously creating herself, "painfully, step by step."

In her 1937 autobiography, Eleanor would be quick to emphasize her youthful transgressions, such as lying about having stolen candy, and slow to give voice to the determination and resolve that shaped her, from a young age, into the most important woman of the twentieth century. She might make passing reference to moments of fearless riding, but not until the end of her life did Eleanor write that in her early childhood "I learned to stare down each of my fears, conquer it, attain the hard-earned courage to go on to the next." Most important, she made it clear that "with each victory, no matter how agonizing it was at the time, I gained increasing confidence."

Years later, her cousin Alice seemed to understand. Her comment was succinct: "I don't think there was any fairy wand."

SOME OF FRANKLIN'S BIOGRAPHERS have given the impression that he had only one or two playmates as a child. But the families who lived on the east bank of the Hudson River spent a lot of time visiting one another, and he often saw his many cousins and his half-niece and half-nephew who lived next door. Helen and Taddy Roosevelt were the children of Franklin's half-brother, James Roosevelt Roosevelt. Good-hearted and effete, twenty-eight years older than Franklin, "Rosy" was the son of James and his first wife, Rebecca, who had died in 1876. Mary Newbold, daughter of the Thomas Jefferson Newbolds, also lived nearby, in a large white house two hundred yards from the Roosevelts'. But a friend remembered Franklin was always trying to "get away" from home and ride his pony down the road to visit his friend Edmund Rogers at Crumwold Hall. From the age of six, he went there every morning for his lessons in the schoolroom with Edmund, and sometimes a boy or two from the village. A neighbor described Franklin, Helen, Mary Newbold, and the Rogers children as a big "cousiny" group that did everything together. Their favorite place to play was Standard Oil executive Colonel Archibald Rogers's seventy-room stone house. Surrounded by green lawns, Crumwold Hall, with its four boys and two girls, was "where all the fun was."

Like Franklin and her cousin Helen, Eleanor went to the Rogerses' house for parties and dancing classes. The children dressed in their best and traveled on a slow train that made special stops for them, house by house. "All through the autumn weeks," Eleanor wrote, the train picked up boys and girls from as far away as "Hudson on the north and Fishkill in the south." After dancing class, the children had their lessons in the Rogerses' schoolroom and ate their supper by the fire before going back home together on the train.

Even when Eleanor and Franklin were older, Crumwold Hall remained the social center for the young people. "Dances during the Christmas holidays; coasting and skating, with tea or supper at this hospitable home . . . were only some of the activities we enjoyed," Eleanor

Eleanor overcame her fear of horses through sheer willpower.

Portrait of Claes Martenszen van Rosenvelt, the first American Roosevelt

Franklin in 1902 with Delano cousins Lyman and (left to right) Catherine, Laura, and Louise

wrote. Friends, her cousin Alice among them, came from New York for house parties. Margaret Dix remembered slipping away from the dancing to go skiing in the moonlight with Franklin, and that he had been "handsome, attractive and awfully nice."

Often in her autobiography, Eleanor's memories are as motionless as children playing the game of statues. But in these other reminiscences, they move, and suddenly it is easy to imagine her running down the parquet floor of Oak Terrace's front hall, autumn light streaming down three stories from the skylight and falling on her in her best dress, eager to be off for a day at Crumwold Hall.

Fourth of July in
Oyster Bay

TEN-YEAR-OLD ELEANOR loved the sentimental novels of
Louisa May Alcott, a taste she shared with her uncle Theodore, who confessed, at the risk of being thought "effeminate," that he had loved them as
a boy. In 1894, Eleanor's life had begun to resemble one of Alcott's stories.
Like Rose in *Eight Cousins,* she had lost both of her parents—and her
brother Elliott Jr. as well. Eleanor's mother had died of diphtheria in 1892,
and her brother's death from the same disease followed in 1893. Her father
collapsed fatally in 1894 from complications of his alcoholism. Like the
orphaned Alcott heroine, Eleanor was drawn to a generous-hearted, book-
ish uncle and a raft of rowdy cousins. Her story would continue to run parallel to Rose's, even to marrying a distant cousin, but fact diverged from
fiction in one significant detail.

　　While Rose got to live with her favorite uncle when her parents
died, Eleanor was delivered into the care of her austere grandmother and a
childhood of borrowed homes. Eleanor once described to a friend what it
had been like "going to live with Auntie 'This' and Auntie 'That' and Grand-

mother 'So-and-So'" and having to be "so polite. Always so excessively polite." It was made clear to the little girl that she "mustn't have any ideas of her own," Frances Perkins said, paraphrasing Eleanor. "She mustn't ask for anything, because, after all, they were taking her in."

Perkins talked about the condescending way the Oyster Bay Roosevelts referred to Eleanor's difficult circumstances. One year the cousins' aunt Corinne Robinson invited Nan Honeyman, a "charming, vigorous, bright gay young girl," to come for Christmas. "Now 'poor little Eleanor' is coming," Corinne briefed Nan. "I want you to be very nice to her. We all try to make Eleanor come for Christmas and have a good time." By Corinne's description, vibrant Nan and "poor little Eleanor" were an ill-starred combination, but the girls took to each other immediately and remained close for many years.

Their friendship would not have surprised Eleanor's schoolmates. She looked like everyone else in her dark blue smock that fell from her shoulders and her yellow hair braided into a thick pigtail. They thought she was one of the group, a girl with "plenty of life and play in her." Like most ten-year-olds, she had her best friends: Jesse Sloane, because she was so pretty, and Helen Cutting, who was everyone's favorite.

What struck Helen Cutting about Eleanor as a child was her sense of "urgency." Years later, reading an essay by Lytton Strachey on Florence Nightingale, Helen said she felt out of breath trying to keep up with the Crimean War nurse. She had seen that same urgency in Eleanor "almost from the beginning."

In the midst of her large and spirited family, Alice felt as orphaned as Eleanor was. Her half-siblings were close in age, and they made a tight-knit group of their own. And although Alice considered Edith her mother, she was told to pray every night for another mother, who lived in heaven. When her younger brother Ted teased Alice about having been breast-fed by a wet nurse after her mother's death, she thought it emphasized the difference between her and the rest of the family. Alice became "hard-minded," as she put it, and learned to "shrug a shoulder with indifference." One day she would say "poor Eleanor" along with the rest of her relatives,

Alice, older and with a different mother, often felt separate from her half-siblings.

The hallway at Sagamore Hill

Theodore and some young Roosevelts playing by the barn at Sagamore Hill

but she didn't say it when the cousins were young. It wasn't Eleanor whom Alice thought lonely and awkward, but herself.

Alice's piano teacher, Emma Knorr, regarded her as "almost a girl from another planet," for beneath her classic features and athletic body lay a precocious and unruly child. Alice insisted on wearing trousers, she talked about wanting twins, and she begged to have a monkey for a pet. She fought with Edith over writing letters and going to school. "I didn't do any of the nice and proper things expected of me," Alice said. She knew that Eleanor did, that her cousin "always made a tremendous effort" to do what was right. But Alice affected not to care. Being thought "selfish and defiant" was preferable to being pitied. Later, Alice said she had had no intention as a child of letting anyone call her a "poor little thing" the way they did Eleanor. And so she went on being difficult, a small, rough creature Theodore and Edith were loath to confront.

"I am so glad Alice is going to be in town this winter," Eleanor wrote her aunt Bye in 1894. She was hoping they would be going to school together every day. But after Elliott's death, Mary Hall wanted her granddaughter to have nothing more to do with the family who had spawned him. Eleanor was no longer even allowed to see her beloved aunt Annie Gracie, because she was considered one of the Oyster Bay clan. Nor did she join Alice, Ted, and Franklin, who, when they spent an occasional winter in the city, often went together to the American Museum of Natural History to hear lectures on birds and look at the exhibits.

Alice's stepmother also tried to separate the cousins, perhaps because she was piqued by Mary Hall's disapproval of her family, and perhaps because Eleanor's father had been a great embarrassment to his Oyster Bay relatives. In the last years of his life, Elliott had maintained mistresses in America and abroad and had fathered an illegitimate son by a servant girl. Born in 1891, this shadow child—Eleanor's half-brother, whom his mother, Catherine Mann, named Elliott Roosevelt Mann—was obviously not welcomed into the Roosevelt family, and few details about his life have been recorded. No doubt Eleanor reminded Edith of a family skeleton potentially harmful to Theodore's political prospects.

In the end, the reasons were unimportant. What mattered was that Edith Roosevelt and Mary Hall each shielded the child in her care from the other child, who was her best friend. "I never wished Alice to associate with Eleanor so shall not try to keep up any friendship between them," Edith told a relative bluntly. Her uncompromising words confirmed Nicholas's belief that while Roosevelts were loyal to family members who conformed to their ideals, they sometimes "ostracized" those who didn't. But despite the wishes of the older women, Eleanor continued to make brief trips to Oyster Bay. She was Theodore's godchild and favorite niece, the vulnerable daughter of his dead brother—more like him, his sister Corinne thought, than any of his own children. Alice waited impatiently for her cousin's annual visit on the Fourth of July.

Franklin, as well, sometimes came for the holiday. He considered a trip to Sagamore Hill a high point of his summer, and one of the few times he challenged his mother openly occurred when she declined on his behalf an invitation to attend Theodore's annual Fourth of July party. "Please don't make any arrangements for my future happiness," fourteen-year-old Franklin told his mother on learning that she had turned down an invitation to Oyster Bay. When Theodore asked him again, "for as long as you can stay," Franklin wrote his mother acidly, "I have accepted Cousin Theodore's invitation and I hope you will not refuse that, too." Sara Roosevelt had mixed feelings about her Long Island relatives. She was fond of them, and she admired Theodore, but the Oyster Bay Roosevelts were "in trade." They were businessmen, not elegant gentleman farmers, as her husband had been.

Theodore had returned to political life after marrying Edith, first serving on the U.S. Civil Service Commission from 1889 to 1895, and then as police commissioner of New York from 1895 to 1897. One of Alice's early memories was the sight of her father leaving for one of his "nocturnal rambles" through the tenement districts. The depression of 1893 had resulted in thousands of business bankruptcies and millions of people were jobless. During a hot spell one summer, Theodore spent most of every night walking the slums, alert to the possibility of riots and listening sympathetically

Theodore taking a fence in 1902

*Theodore and Edith hiking with the children
in Oyster Bay*

Young Ted on a hunting trip

to the needs of the inhabitants. "It is an excellent thing to have rapid transit," Theodore reported, but it was more important to have "ample playgrounds" in the poor sections of the city.

At the end of each week, Theodore returned to Sagamore Hill, and family meals were crowded with relatives and guests. His eldest son, Ted, said later that from the age of nine he had listened to his father and his friends talk about social change. Eleanor first heard the word *politics* at the Sagamore dining room table, and Alice would not remember a time when she had not known about politics and politicians.

By 1894, the band of cousins had diminished in number. J. West had lost one son, Harold, in April 1892, and three months later a second, Lewis; like Eleanor's brother Elliott in 1893, they probably died from diphtheria. Still, some fourteen young Roosevelts often ranged across Oyster Bay, considering it their private preserve. Sometimes they ate several breakfasts in the course of a single morning, appearing at J. West's for one, at Emlen's for another, and at Sagamore Hill for a third.

Theodore's "tribal affection," as Alice called it, embraced the Roosevelt cousins. His niece Corinne—hereafter referred to as Corinne Jr. in order to distinguish her from her mother—said he had loved them from the time they were "tiny babies." A near maternal tenderness drew the children close to Theodore, and his kindness made them want to be like him.

When the cousins grew older, he was a door flung wide. A picnic with Theodore was always on the farthest island by way of the smallest rowboat on the hottest day. Any adventure served, as long as it was difficult. He might decide the family should go down Cooper's Bluff, a precipitous two-hundred-foot drop of sand that ended at the beach below. A dozen Roosevelt children would lash themselves together, hand to hand according to size and age, and all of them would stand or fall together, with Theodore urging them on, the smallest and youngest first, running and stumbling in a pack until they reached the bottom of the bluff at the edge of the bay. More than forty years later, at a White House press conference, Eleanor and Franklin would interrupt each other in their eagerness to tell reporters just how frightened they had been.

Eleanor was "desperately afraid" her first time down Cooper's Bluff, but by her second run she had mastered her fear, unlike Alice, who, "rather chunky and not a little cowardly," swung at the end of the whip of squealing cousins. "Oh, those perfectly awful endurance tests masquerading as games!" Alice said years later. She was also scared to ride horseback and scared to dive. Her family claimed there was a perceptible rise in the tide every time she tried. "My cousin Eleanor was always so fine about that sort of thing," Alice said. "She hated it as much as I did but was much more unprotesting."

Outside the barn, Theodore stood with a stopwatch in his hand and exhorted the children to run their fastest in races across the hay, the girls in short, dirty dresses and the boys in overalls and old tennis shoes. Franklin's Oyster Bay cousins maintained later that he had not been good at the games the children played. Corinne Jr. recalled that his tennis was lousy, though the mice who frisked across the Sagamore court in the middle of the action and the low branches that lay in wait for the lobs of the uninitiated might have made it an unfair game. Franklin had known how to ride and dive and swim since childhood. On Campobello he challenged friends to hike the bouldered shoreline, and they sometimes turned back even before they reached the stretch that had to be swum through eddies that tossed waves high over rocks. As a teenager, he was caught with a friend in a birch-bark canoe in a storm, and they spent the night fighting currents that were dangerous on even the calmest day.

Alice's scrappy brother Ted, five years younger than Franklin, tried to beat his cousin in every sport. His behavior was unaffected by the fact that, like Franklin, he had worn kilts as a little boy. Small for his age and competitive, young Ted wanted nothing so much as to win, and please his father.

Theodore's thesis at Harvard had argued for women's equality, and he expected the girls as well as the boys to scramble across the hay and run down Cooper's Bluff. The cousins did not realize that Theodore was pushing them to excel in part because his own ceaseless "striving" helped him keep his ghosts at bay. The children were too young to understand what

Theodore meant when he said "black care" rarely sat behind a rider whose pace was fast enough. They knew nothing of his pain—his sadness over his first wife's death, his guilt over marrying a second time—but they found possibilities for themselves in his example. He had labored long in his own creation, and they thought they could make themselves too, the girls no less than the boys.

"I think I must have a good deal of my uncle Theodore Roosevelt in me," Eleanor wrote years later, "because I enjoy a good fight." Sheer grit was the building block of her personality, as it was of his. Their philosophies were so similar that, writing about happiness, Theodore observed that it came as a "by-product of striving to do what must be done," while Eleanor would write that happiness was nothing in itself, nothing more than a "by-product" of doing things for other people.

In the afternoons, the cousins climbed the stairs to the gun room, where, while Theodore quoted poetry, they gazed with interest at the fang marks a mountain lion had bitten into his .30-.30 Winchester rifle butt. Sometimes he paused to repeat a verse that pleased him, and Eleanor learned those parts by heart, for her uncle was the man "whose admiration I craved." Like Eleanor, Franklin watched Theodore carefully. He too craved his cousin's admiration, and he followed his example. But his motivation was competition. A friend said later that the most important force driving Franklin was his determination to "outshine" not young Ted but his older cousin Theodore.

On the Fourth of July, the village of Oyster Bay draped red, white, and blue banners on the bandstand amid the old apple trees at the edge of the bay. Theodore had climbed the trees as a boy to listen to the band play and the men give speeches. Now it was he who stood amid the bright flags and spoke to the townsfolk and his children, nieces, and nephews. For rich and poor alike, the clan solidarity Theodore represented was important at the turn of the century. From poor families, who could survive only by living and working together, to the Hapsburgs, who had joined all of Europe with an intricate tracery of marriage ties, a united family was both the Victorian ideal and the key to survival. In Oyster Bay, the Roosevelt cousins shinnied up the apple trees and listened as Theodore called on them to improve the living and working conditions for the families in the tenements thirty miles away. In the evening, they watched the fireworks from the grassy western slope of Sagamore Hill. For two hours rockets and pinwheels shot color into the darkness, and one year a portrait of Theodore hung fleetingly above the family gathered on the lawn. The cousins never forgot their summer weekends with him, his personality as large by day over the fields of Oyster Bay as his smile that played across the night sky.

American War, and now worked for the Astor Trust. "As soon as he saw me," Eleanor wrote in 1961, he "came over and asked me to dance." A number of Ferguson's friends and co-workers at the Trust invited her as well, among them Duncan Harris, Pendleton Rogers, and Nicholas Biddle. Harris remembered Eleanor as an "interesting talker," and Alice would describe her as an intellectual who liked to discuss whether "contentment was better than happiness and whether they conflicted." But the friendships also had their frivolous side. One afternoon the ordinarily grave Ferguson came to Eleanor's for tea with Nick Biddle and Otway Bird, and they behaved like unruly boys, banging on tom-toms, talking like Indians, and telephoning all of her friends.

Dancing masters complained of seeing the same casual attitude at the New York balls. They said that young men clasped girls' hands to their chests in unheard-of intimacy, and that their bows to their partners were brief and perfunctory. Dance steps were inexact, often sloppy, and girls drew their skirts immodestly to their hips. People wondered what was to become of the old ways, but at the Assembly Ball, as always, the cotillion— a long dance made up of shorter dances called figures—remained as formal as ever. A newspaper remarked that the cousins were a pretty sight, dancing in the same figure. Between dances they gossiped on the gilt chairs that lined the yellow ballroom.

Alice's large black leather Clayton's Quarto diary recorded that she enjoyed herself at the Assembly Ball. Her entries often contained reports of having had "a great old time," but they also showed a girl whose self-assurance was glass thin. Alice wrote of herself as "nondescript"; she wished she were "a most marvellous belle and more run after than any other girl." One afternoon, no one at all had come to see her while on another, fifteen men had paid calls on her cousin Christine. "I don't think I ever make an impression on anybody," Alice confessed. The night of the Assembly Ball, along with her report of having had "a great old time," she wrote, "Arthur was not there." Alice was sure that Arthur Iselin would become engaged to someone else. "I pray God make him love me Arthur Arthur my love and my life."

Franklin had not come to the ball either. Eleanor knew she could count on him to dance with her at parties, but she realized, sadly, that he "wasn't always there." As an editor of the *Harvard Crimson,* Franklin had to remain in Cambridge that night, staying up late to work with the printers and get out the newspaper.

In the days after the ball, Eleanor and Alice continued to call on friends together and attend the formal dances and dinner parties that took place nearly every evening. On December 30, one of Eleanor's aunts gave her a theater party. Sixty-six young people attended the play *Cavalier* and the dinner and dancing that followed at Sherry's. An old classmate remarked that Eleanor's friends were the same ones she had before she went to Allenswood, only the group was "bigger." The cousins' aunt Corinne wrote her daughter that she had attended the play that evening just to watch the "great theatre party" of cousins and friends come in, and had found it "very jolly."

When Alice and Eleanor had free moments, they spent them together. They lunched at Eleanor's house, spent a quiet afternoon reading novels, hunted for a fortune-teller, and dropped by the Café Martin after a morning of shopping. One day, in an undated entry in her 1902 diary, Alice carefully set down the names of the twenty-seven boys and girls "with whom I should like to go into seclusion at a convent or a ranch." The name at the top of her list was Eleanor's.

THRESHOLDS

1902–1906

White House New Year

ON DECEMBER 31, 1902, Eleanor, Alice, their cousin Christine, Margaret Dix, and Richard Derby arrived in Washington by train from New York. Nearly a dozen young New Yorkers, Franklin among them, had been invited to spend several days in the capital attending receptions, balls, dinners, and plays as guests of the president and his family. That afternoon, Franklin had tea with Alice and Eleanor in the White House before they separated to go on to different New Year's Eve parties.

The young visitors smelled turpentine when they walked through the White House, and paint cloths covered the floors in some of the rooms. Edith was restoring the eighteenth-century building to its Federal simplicity. It had been full of Victorian dark mahogany, ornate wallpapers, and potted palms, and now she was redecorating the rooms with buff and white paint, light, elegant furniture, and fresh flowers. "Only a yahoo," Theodore said, "could have his taste offended." His daughter's was: Alice called the renovations "hideous."

When Edith began her work, massive greenhouses had obscured an airy colonnade designed by Thomas Jefferson. Now the graceful curve of slender columns led from the White House to the new West Wing, built to contain the administrative offices. For years, the clerks and their clanking typewriters, spittoons, ink pots, and wastebaskets had disturbed the family in their quarters nearby; they had made it, novelist Owen Wister commented, "a nasty place to be."

But the casual zoo that presided over the family breakfast table remained. Thirteen-year-old Kermit often fed his pet kangaroo rat sugar cubes on the damask cloth while his father poured coffee for their guests, and Alice was likely to wander in with her pet snake wrapped around her arm. The list of animals residing in the White House was exotic and ever-shifting. When Alice was away, her stepmother reported that the ferret was thriving; and on a trip to Florida, she had written the children that she had found a shop where she could buy the alligators they wanted. Quentin, the youngest Roosevelt boy, even brought a Shetland pony named Algonquin up the elevator and into Archie's room when his brother was sick with diphtheria. A parrot and a blue macaw were also part of the family's menagerie, and chief usher Ike Hoover thought a nervous person had no business around the White House those days.

Meanwhile, Theodore ate his grapefruit and told amusing stories. A favorite was about the day he and the French ambassador, Jean-Jules Jusserand, decided to go swimming in the Potomac. They walked to the edge of the river, beyond the view of houses and streetcars, then stripped and swam across with their clothes piled on top of their heads. Except for the formal gray gloves Jusserand was still wearing. When the ambassador and the president emerged, naked and dripping, on the Virginia bank of the Potomac, Jusserand explained, "I thought we might meet the ladies."

The president's warmth and humor engaged family and friends alike; only Alice's fifteen-year-old brother was "sick and tired" of life in the White House. Young Ted complained that it was a handicap to be Theodore's son, to have to carry his name. Alice thought things were "complicated" for him, and Theodore worried about his eldest son, "everlastingly having sanguinary battles with outsiders."

In the evenings, Alice and her houseguests dined on the creamy English Wedgwood Edith had commissioned, its pattern incorporating the Great Seal in a colonial motif in red, gold, and brown. The controversial

*Theodore's sons
Archie and Quentin
Roosevelt, with a
line-up of policemen
on the White House
grounds*

*Alice and her
brother Quentin
playing catch
on the White
House lawn*

*The newly constructed
West Wing of the White
House about 1902*

painting *Love and Life* was back on the wall. Years before, President Grover Cleveland had taken down the picture of two nudes at the request of the Women's Christian Temperance Union. Theodore had reinstated the painting, and the WCTU's National Superintendent of Purity in Literature and Art was again calling for its removal. But on New Year's Eve, the State Dining Room was resplendent with David Watts's lusty nudes in their "atrocious postures."

The next day the doors of the White House were open to the public. The Red Room glowed patriotically, and the gold stars on the curtains in the Blue Room caught the sun as Theodore and Edith stood at the head of the receiving line, greeting well-wishers. The president was delighted to see the citizens of America on the first day of 1903. His vow to protect their individual rights was the cornerstone of his presidency.

It was a heady experience for Franklin to stand near the president in what he called the "inner circle." He had turned to Theodore after his father's death in 1900, and following his example, he was working at Harvard for the common good. Franklin had raised money that year for a relief fund for the Boers in their struggle against Britain for an independent South Africa.

Boston newspapers described him as being like his cousin, hardworking and democratic, and they wrote that he was among the first to suggest a student pro-Boer movement. Franklin's example had quickly been followed on other university campuses. That fall, his friend Edmund Rogers arranged for him to speak at Yale—Harvard's traditional rival—and Franklin told the students that "competition is good in its place, but its place is here at college." After they graduated, he said, he hoped they would all work together for those "who have had less opportunity than we." Even though Franklin gave his speech during the weekend of the Yale-Harvard football game, the hundred Yale men cheered him.

Franklin spent some time with Eleanor during their holiday in Washington. When he mentioned in his journal that he sat near her one afternoon at the theater, his brief entry was prophetic. For the rest of his life, Franklin would talk about the willowy adolescent seated next to him at dinner parties and plays during the winter of 1902.

Despite Franklin's interest in Eleanor, her relatives noticed that she was withdrawn. The White House was a dazzling scene on New Year's Day as Army officers decked with medals filed past and the Marine band played passages from Mascagni's *Cavalleria Rusticana*. But suddenly Eleanor and a few other houseguests left Alice and Franklin behind in the receiving line and went out for a walk. The next night, Eleanor and Margaret Dix decided not to attend a charity ball, and Alice had to go without them. Another day Eleanor told Theodore and Edith she didn't want to receive at the Admiral of the Navy's, and they were disappointed that she took so little interest in things American.

The cousins' aunt Corinne was concerned about Eleanor's behavior. Her niece could not afford to offend her Oyster Bay relatives. A young orphaned girl, Corinne felt, needed family support; she blamed Eleanor's behavior on the unstable life she led with her aunt Pussie. Eleanor claimed later to have been overawed by the pomp and pageantry of the White House, but her life just then was very difficult. That spring Corinne would write, "Eleanor came to see me. . . . She burst into tears and said 'Auntie, I have no *real* home,' in such a pathetic way that my heart simply ached for her." One day Eleanor would say that her experiences that winter "hardened me in much the way that steel is tempered."

There may have been another reason that Eleanor seemed defensive on her visit to the White House. Perhaps she did not know that Edith tried to separate her and Alice, but she may have sensed her aunt's continuing disapproval of their friendship. After that visit, Eleanor stayed with her aunt Bye when she came to Washington; she explained that she felt more comfortable there.

Alice's seeming self-assurance contrasted sharply with Eleanor's withdrawal. But while Alice flirted and danced until all hours and relatives noted men "seven deep" around her, she was writing over and over in her diary, "I am an absolute fool. Couldn't get along. Felt stiff and affected."

*Alice's fondness for birds and animals was a
Roosevelt family trait.*

*Young Ted preferred Sagamore Hill and did not
like life in the White House.*

Two friends visited her in January, and when they left, she wrote wistfully how much everyone had liked them. "No hope for Alice," she noted, many times. Her entries listed the men in her life, at first a few, then many more, but she felt little confidence with any of them. Gherardesca—a "heartless Latin"—left Alice tongue-tied and furious with herself. Her passions seemed both relentless and futile, and though the names changed, the refrain remained the same: "John John John," she wrote of John Greenway. "If you would care for me."

Every once in a while, the insecurities that Alice recorded secretly came briefly out in the open. Over tea with Edith, she wept and admitted she didn't think her father loved her "one eighth as much as his other children." Although Alice tried to rationalize later, in her diary, that she did not care "overmuch" for him anyway, finally the truth spilled out. "Heaven knows," she wrote, "I am perfectly well aware that I haven't got it in my commonplace self to love anyone overmuch, except Alice, but I certainly do love him with all the love that I am so far capable of." Nonetheless, she quickly resumed her habit of defiance, to conceal how unloved she felt. As a child Alice had stamped her foot and refused to go to school. Now she slept late, sometimes all day long. When a friend asked Theodore why he didn't look after her more, he answered famously, "I can be President of the United States—or—I can attend to Alice." Corinne was as disturbed about this niece as she was about Eleanor. She "deplored" the way Alice needed to be the center of attention, "always madly gay or bored to death."

Edith, too, criticized Alice, who catalogued her stepmother's reproaches in her diary: She was selfish and cared for no one but herself; she was far too interested in money and fast cars; she had no friends and did not spend enough time with her family. Though Alice gave her stepmother ample reason to find fault, the criticisms seem excessive. Edith's comments to other family members could be harsh, but they were rarely more devastating—or more frequent—than those she directed at her stepdaughter.

Long ago, Alice had learned to protect herself from the pain of her father's absences by appearing not to care. But she had also learned to armor herself against Edith's complex feelings toward the girl who looked just like Theodore's dead wife. When her stepmother accused her of wearing a "queer wicked expression," Alice bragged in her diary that it had been perfected over months of practice. And yet sometimes, castigating herself for her behavior, she promised to do better. Until then, the landlocked present contained her outward, warring attributes—arrogance and charm, anger and warmth—as well as her inner fears. Like Eleanor, Alice was caught between a troubled past and an unknown future.

First Steps

BIOGRAPHERS SOMETIMES CITE the summer of 1903 as the beginning of Franklin's serious courtship of Eleanor; it actually appears to have started during the winter of her debutante season, six months earlier. The evidence is misleading: In his pocket journal Franklin noted only that he had tea and lunch with Eleanor in December and that she was a guest at his twenty-first-birthday party a month later. Other than an allusion to her presence on their trip to Washington, she isn't mentioned. Nor does Eleanor's autobiography suggest their courtship started in earnest that winter.

But near the end of her life, Eleanor described in some detail the afternoons and evenings she and Franklin spent together when he "began coming to see me during my first winter back in New York." She wrote: "I found myself looking forward eagerly to seeing Franklin." One reason his presence in the household escaped comment was that they were cousins, and had known each other since childhood. At the age of seven, thanking his godfather, Elliott Roosevelt, for the seal ring he would use "when I am a man," Franklin had asked him to "send my love" to Eleanor.

No unmarried young girl in those days was ever alone with a suitor; when someone called on Eleanor, her aunt stayed nearby to chaperone.

But when Franklin visited her "during the year Pussie and I lived together," Eleanor wrote, she did not even bother to come downstairs. Eleanor was "amazed" that their family connection allowed them to see each other without the usual restrictions. As a result, she and Franklin "knew and liked each other first as friends who enjoyed being together."

"Another thing that helped us was Bob Ferguson's friendship," Eleanor wrote of the man who had looked out for her at the Assembly Ball. "He was literally my good angel." Loved and trusted by the Roosevelt family, and by the Halls as well, Ferguson met Mary Hall's requirements for being a chaperone. Eleanor, Franklin, and Bob talked about books, went to parties together, and visited friends in Greenwich Village. The bohemian section of the city, with its foreign restaurants and fifty-cent dinners, beer gardens and aspiring writers, was a community in revolt. The "new literature" was much discussed, for novelists Theodore Dreiser, Upton Sinclair, and Sinclair Lewis were exploring the lives of the working poor. Their books were given added currency by the recent conclusion of one investigation commission that conditions in America's cities were worse than they had been a half-century before.

Because they spent so much time together, Eleanor's friends actually thought it was Bob who wished to mean something more to her. But though they shared a love of books, she dismissed him on the grounds of his being "much older"—by fourteen years—than she. Eventually Ferguson married Isabella Selmes, one of Eleanor's closest friends.

The conventions of New York society also camouflaged Franklin's interest in Eleanor. On Tuesday afternoons, residents of the houses along Fifth Avenue were expected to be "at home" to receive visitors. Wednesday afternoons were reserved for the residents of Lexington Avenue and Park Avenue, and for those with addresses east and west of Fifth Avenue from Twenty-third Street to Fiftieth Street. Friends could call uninvited at 11 West 37th Street on that day, so no one paid much attention if Franklin dropped by.

Eleanor later gave the impression that she and Pussie had had few visitors during the winter of 1902–1903. Probably the emotional truth of her life—the loneliness she felt because of the loss of her parents and brother, and her difficulties with Pussie and Vallie—clouded the actual facts. Guests often stopped in for tea and were invited to luncheons and dinners.

All Eleanor's life, her aunts had given parties, and they "took it for granted that I would come to their social affairs." Pussie liked to entertain in the billiard room on her good days, and one of Eleanor's friends remembered being "fascinated" by the room downstairs that swelled with laughter and music. Someone was always playing the piano and singing from the latest song sheets, while Pussie, ravishingly beautiful, flirted with the men who came to call. However erratic she was in other ways, she always drew a shy man into conversation, and Eleanor inherited her social gifts. At Allenswood the English girls left new foreign students in a corner, Marie Souvestre wrote; she had counted on Eleanor to make them "feel rapidly at ease."

There were no "dreadful silences" when Franklin called, Eleanor reported. She was "never uncomfortable with the college friends whom he often brought with him." They were enthusiastic about a young professor, Charles Townsend Copeland, who spent evenings with them in Cambridge discussing literature. Eleanor liked to talk about "Copey's" latest recommendations, and she made her own suggestions to Franklin, among them Balzac's *La Peau de chagrin,* and Ruskin's *Sesame and Lilies.* Years later, Eleanor wrote that she fell in love with Franklin because he liked to read as much as she did.

A sociable man even in his intellectual pursuits, Franklin told a friend that he preferred reading aloud to someone else to reading silently to himself. He enjoyed criticizing a novel Eleanor liked, so that he could watch her "leap heatedly" into a discussion. Though they both loved Dickens, they disagreed about their favorite characters. Harvard friends criticized Franklin for being argumentative, but Eleanor liked his "Dutch obstinacy" and the "set look of his jaw."

Franklin taught Eleanor to evaluate whether an author was "reliable" and knew what he was "talking about." She remembered his "always asking me 'Why?,'" and often she hurried to the library to be better prepared the next time they met. When Franklin and Eleanor had been married for a long time, he would proudly advise a friend not to argue with "the Missus," because "you think you have her pinned down here"—thumping the table with his forefinger—"but she bobs up right away over there somewhere! No use—you can't win."

A powerful family style guided Eleanor in her relationship with Franklin. Since childhood she had listened to her uncle Theodore discussing politics, literature, and art with his sisters. "Uncle Ted had his firm opinions and so did my aunts," Eleanor remembered. But while their conversations "frequently became emphatic," they were "never acrimonious." A family retainer would have the same recollection of Theodore and his wife. They argued over almost everything, but "always amiably."

Sometimes Eleanor's eleven-year-old brother, Hall, joined the group for tea. He had been a baby when their parents died and left him in their grandmother's care. But Mary Hall was distant and austere, preferring to spend most of her time alone in her bedroom. Eleanor treated Hall as her son, writing him letters often when he was away at school, so that he would know he "belongs" to someone. As a teenager, Hall took a sailing trip with Franklin, who steered them for hours through a dangerous gale. Hall wrote later that his brother-in-law's back looked solid and dependable as he stood at the bow "clenching and unclenching his cramped hands" when the storm finally let up. He was astonished, when Franklin turned around, by the joy that lighted his face, the total absence of fear. In 1903, the fatherless boy no doubt found Franklin's presence comforting. Hall was frightened of his uncle Vallie's drunken appearances and disturbed by Pussie's tantrums.

SEVERAL MONTHS AFTER Franklin began courting Eleanor, a cheer went up on the Brooklyn piers when Alice paused on her way up a gangplank and turned to the crowd with a smile that reminded one reporter of her father's. Theodore's muscular grin was caricatured end-

Franklin was slow to tell his mother, Sara, about his courtship of Eleanor.

Franklin and Hall sailing with friends at Campobello in 1906

Usually Alice refused to smile for the camera, not wishing to be caricatured as her father was with his signature grin.

lessly, and she had perfected a nearly sullen expression to avoid his fate. But on March 14, 1903, nineteen-year-old Alice smiled. She was about to sail for Puerto Rico, newly won by the United States in the recent war against Spain.

The night before, after a family party, Alice had gone to the opera with Eleanor, Helen, and Teddy Robinson. A relative wrote that they had a "thoroughly good time" and that their "box was jammed" with friends all evening. But now, after Helen and Teddy had seen her off at the pier, Alice was alone with her maid. Although Theodore had tried to persuade her to take along a companion, the newspapers wrote, she said she wanted "all the freedom possible."

Alice had traveled to Cuba the year before. Lodged in the house of the American ambassador, she had fulfilled her duties by day, but at night she had carried on with one young diplomat after another. And while she had confessed her shame to her diary, when confronted by her host, Theodore's friend General Leonard Wood, she had responded defiantly. On the trip to Puerto Rico, the pressure on Alice to behave would be considerable. The press was scrutinizing her conduct as Theodore prepared for the presidential election in November. If a photograph had been taken from halfway up Pacific Street that day, it would have exposed the relentlessly public quality of Alice's life. In her dark suit and high-necked white blouse, she looked like any other Victorian girl in a box of family photographs—except for her admirers milling around the pier where the *Coamo* was docked, and the dozen policemen and several detectives assigned to protect her.

In Puerto Rico, thousands of people crowded into San Juan's central plaza, hanging out over balconies and edging along rooftops to catch a glimpse of Alice. There were receptions, fetes, and dinners in her honor. The governor of the island, William Hunt, invited seven hundred guests to tea. She toured the nucleus of the new University of Puerto Rico with the island's commissioner of education and reviewed the troops at the barracks of Morro Castle. On her four-day trip into the interior, Alice's train was decorated with palm trees and flags, and she sat on a straight-backed chair on an open flatcar, the life and scent of the rain forest an arm's length away.

Alice reveled in the sensuous tropical island, but unlike on her trip to Cuba, this time she was mature enough to take her responsibilities seriously. Everywhere she went—to Cayey, Ponce, Mayagüez, and the great sugar plantations—she said and did the right thing. The demands of diplomacy suited Alice. At home her need for new experiences drove her beyond the limits of what was considered acceptable; here it fueled her interest in the Puerto Rican people. Her impulsive nature, a liability in her social world, made her a flexible traveler. "Don't speak of my going away," she told reporters. "I don't like to think of it."

On the day of Alice's departure, bands played and salutes were fired from the German and Italian warships docked in the turquoise waters of San Juan harbor. The ships dipped their colors as the *Coamo* steamed past, and Alice waved goodbye with a white lace handkerchief. Her fellow passengers reported that she was the life of the ship and the most accomplished pianist on board. Even the chief steward had a compliment: He reported after a day of heavy swells that she had been the best sailor on the passenger list. "Everyone has been so kind to me," Alice said.

Theodore was impressed. "Darling Alice," he wrote. "You were of real service down there because you made those people feel that you liked them and took an interest in them, and your presence was accepted as a great compliment." But once back home, his daughter fidgeted. He had taught her to compete, with heated chases down Cooper's Bluff and intellectual discussions around the breakfast table, but what had it all been for? "Oh no one knows how *very* much I should like to really count in all the big things," Alice wrote in her diary. She papered over her frustration with social excess, accepting more and more invitations to parties given by ever-richer friends, all the while considering herself a "perfect ass."

Wherever Alice looked, her family seemed to be leading better lives than she. Watching her sister, Ethel, sit for the first time astride a pony, she confessed a wish that the younger girl were not so beguiling. Eleanor's charity work pleased Theodore, and he took Alice to task for gallivanting with "society" rather than spending time with people like her cousin. Sometimes Alice agreed. "Look at you," she said wryly to her father. "Six children. Five splendid torch bearers and one will-o'-the-wisp."

Early in the summer of 1903, Alice and Eleanor visited their aunt Bye at her white clapboard country house, Oldgate, in Farmington, Connecticut. Over the next five days, Alice mentioned Eleanor ten times in her diary. She described their hours in canoes on the Connecticut River and in carriages over the sunny hills, as synchronized as the hands on companion clocks. One moment they were visiting friends, and the next they were both sick—Eleanor "rather seedy" with a bad cold and Alice weathering her third attack of nervous indigestion. Nearly every evening, Alice wrote, they talked together at length—"about us and our respective families and lives."

Among the other houseguests was the cousins' friend Jean Reid, who had helped found the Junior League, a group of young society women committed to working with the poor. Eleanor was visiting crippled children at the Orthopedic Hospital—founded by her grandfather Theodore Sr.— one day a week, and she was interested in Jean's work at the Rivington Street Settlement House. Alice noted in her diary that the three girls discussed "everything and eternity," but what struck her was the sense of social responsibility shared by the other two: "They have very good minds—decidedly religious." Several months later, Alice wrote of wishing that a change would come over her ideas, that she too would emerge "full of high and noble thoughts, stirrings and ideas."

In the meantime, at loose ends, Alice grasped at love. "Oh if only Arthur had loved me," the refrain went in her diary of one of her old loves, long after she had stopped caring. But at the same moment, she acknowledged that she didn't know what the word *love* "really" meant, and wondered if she ever would. Given the brevity of her affections, marriage was proving elusive.

Vows

ON JUNE 18, 1904, bells tolled in St. James Church in Hyde Park as a large carriage drew up. Clouds of bridesmaids in white muslin dresses and white straw garden hats, Alice and Eleanor among them, billowed out. The bride, her chiffon train transparent in the noon sun, was Helen Roosevelt.

Inside the little stone church, squares of watercolor sky rippled behind old glass, and the scent of roses hung thickly, but newspapers covering the wedding took no note of the romantic setting or the fragrant flowers. Instead, a reporter wrote that the air was "filled with Roosevelts" and that the guest list had been gone over by a committee of three "until all undesirable elements" had been "weeded out." It is impossible to know the truth of a committee pulling out undesirables like so many dandelions, but the wedding, as one paper commented, was as "exclusive" as anyone could wish.

The newspapers dwelled on the "long-looked-forward-to and much-heralded Roosevelt-Robinson wedding," for the marriage represented a uniting of the Roosevelt clan. Helen, the daughter of Franklin's half-brother, Rosy, was a descendant of Jacobus Roosevelt. The groom was her sixth cousin Teddy Robinson, whose ancestor was Johannes Roosevelt.

Young cousins from both branches of the family were bridesmaids and ushers.

All of the Roosevelts had made an effort to attend, but Theodore's journey from Washington to Hyde Park had been the most complicated. In order to arrive in time for the noon ceremony, the presidential railroad car, the *Mayflower,* had to be coupled the night before to a Pennsylvania Railroad train, which pulled into Jersey City at five-thirty the morning of the wedding. The *Mayflower* and the president had then been floated up the Hudson River on a transfer boat owned by the New York, New Haven, and Hartford Railways. At Harlem, the *Mayflower* was attached to a New York Central locomotive for the last leg of the trip, up through the Hudson Highlands to Hyde Park.

In later years, Alice liked to say that the difference between her family and Franklin's was that hers had traveled in a borrowed railroad car while his had owned one. It wasn't that Alice's family was poor. It was that, as Theodore put it, he had inherited enough money to give his children bread, but he had to earn the money to give them jam. Although Franklin's family had money for both bread and jam, his situation was similar to Theodore's. Franklin's mother, Sara, controlled the family purse strings, and he cultivated habits of frugality partly to avoid having to ask her for money. He wore his father's suits for thirty years and later his sons' cast-off clothing. He claimed to think restaurants were a waste of money, and his children rarely ate in them until they were grown.

Sara Roosevelt, sitting in her pew and listening to the marriage vows, no doubt recalled her own wedding day, when James had brought her home to Hyde Park. The colors of the sunset had glazed the waters of the Hudson as their carriage made its way along the river road, and every morning that first summer, she and her husband had cut basketsful of roses in their garden before breakfast. She hoped Franklin would settle down to the same quiet life in the valley.

Given the rural setting of the little church and the array of cousins, Theodore may have mused over the new "scramble walk" he was planning for them. Wearing "as few old clothes as possible," he had just written his

Helen and her husband, Teddy Robinson (center), with the bridal party. From left: Corinne Jr. (fourth), Mary Newbold (sixth), Alice (eighth). From right: Eleanor (fourth) and Franklin (fifth)

Franklin, Sara, and Eleanor in Newburgh, New York, 1905

Franklin sailing at Campobello

son Kermit, first they would hike through the woods near Sagamore Hill, swim across the pond in their clothes, and make their way to Cold Spring Harbor, where they would swim diagonally to a cousin's beach, wade through the marsh—preferably, he thought, at high tide—and, finally, go "straight to our several homes to get clean and dry." Theodore was fond of this game of follow-the-leader, where the cousins were required to go over or under or through an obstacle, but never around it. He considered it an excellent exercise in physical courage.

After the ceremony, the bride and groom, the bridesmaids and the ushers, and the guests danced the Virginia reel on the lawn. The wedding breakfast was served under a canopy on tables put together in the shape of a horseshoe for good luck. Everyone threw rice at Helen and Teddy, and when the guests said goodbye, some of them knew that, less than a month later, they would be reunited in Dark Harbor, Maine, in the summer homes of relatives and friends. When Franklin moored his yacht, the *Half Moon*, in a nearby bay one morning in July, Corinne Jr. couldn't tell whether his visit made Eleanor happy or not. Finally she decided that he was "very crazy about her but she not about him. It is truly pathetic." She worried that Eleanor was being insensitive. "I feel very badly for Franklin," Corinne Jr. confessed, "that she really doesn't love him!"

The truth was that Eleanor and Franklin had been secretly engaged for several months, but they had promised his mother not to make the announcement until Thanksgiving. Twenty-two-year-old Franklin sensed the hope implicit in Sara's request—that their engagement would not survive the secret year. He knew that his mother thought he was too young to marry, and that she wanted to keep him to herself for a bit longer. But Franklin was in love. He had chosen to enter Columbia Law School because he wanted to be near Eleanor; he would wait, but not without her. And he had made it clear by visiting Hall, who was newly installed at the Groton School, that he would share Eleanor's family responsibilities. Although Franklin had bowed to his mother's wish not to announce their engagement until November, he had not hidden his love as resolutely as Eleanor hid hers. She had kept her promise to Sara so well that neither

Corinne Jr. nor Alice had discerned the truth. In fact, Alice teased Eleanor about liking Franklin's Harvard roommate, Lathrop Brown.

Corinne Jr.'s diary entries that summer recorded none of the negative feelings she later professed to have had about Franklin. One day she would tell younger family members that he hadn't been the kind of boy to make attractive friends, but in 1904, she thought it was "very nice" to see Franklin. In Maine in midsummer, magenta spikes of wild phlox burst into a sunny sky. Corinne Jr. wrote that the weather on July 20 was "marvellous" when she and Eleanor and some thirty other young people boated and drove six miles to a bluff overlooking the ocean, where Franklin and his friend Jack Minturn gave "a grand party."

House parties were also occasions for quiet conversations, and in the afternoons, Eleanor and Corinne Jr., curled up on summer beds, read and discussed Robert Browning's *Pippa Passes*. The cousins were like-minded in their intellectual interests, but Eleanor would also take the time to allay the younger girl's fears about her coming Assembly Ball. Corinne Jr. admired this cousin. At another house party, in another quiet bedroom, she and several relatives would talk one day about "Eleanor Roosevelt's character" and the "difference between unconventionality and conventionality of spirit." For the family was aware that she was showing increasing signs of independence. When Mary Hall decided not to keep up their brownstone, Eleanor told a friend years later that she had "wanted to live alone." But, unable to overcome her family's resistance, she had gone instead to stay on East Seventy-sixth Street with her cousin Susie Parish. Despite Eleanor's disappointment, Susie was pleased to see her taking a "great interest in people."

Eleanor had joined the Consumer's League and become familiar with legislation that could improve the lives of poor families. More important, she later wrote, "I entered my first sweatshop and walked up the steps of my first tenement." There she saw young children of four or five working at tables "until they dropped with fatigue. . . ." She proved an effective member of the Junior League, working with Jean Reid at the Rivington Street Settlement House, two blocks south of Houston Street. Franklin

Eleanor at the time
of her courtship

In the summer of 1904, Franklin's courtship of
Eleanor was in full swing.

Franklin (left) and Hall
in a tent at Campobello

Franklin and Eleanor at Campobello Island in 1904

sometimes picked her up there. He was the leader of St. Andrews Boys Club, in a poor section of Boston—"and very much interested," Eleanor later wrote, "in his boys and their families." But when he carried one of her sick young students up the steps of a New York City tenement house, Franklin told her, "My God, I didn't know people lived like that!"

Eleanor had also paid long visits to her aunt Bye in Washington, at the house she owned on N Street. She saw her uncle Theodore often, for he invited her to dine at the White House and stopped by to talk about politics and literature with Bye. That winter Eleanor was reading the missionary A. H. Smith's work, *Chinese Characteristics,* no doubt because Theodore was discussing, on his visits to the N Street house, the onset in the Far East of the Russo-Japanese War. Theodore was mindful of the possibility of American involvement, and he was concerned that lives were being lost to "cold steel," despite the fact that sword carrying had begun to seem ceremonial at the turn of the century. He told the War Department that American officers wearing swords ought to be able to "cut and thrust" with them. After a committee review, the department ordered that swordsmanship continue to be taught at the military academies.

Such realities affected Eleanor personally as she poured at Bye's English-style tea hour. Nick Biddle was sometimes among the guests, and she told Franklin that she was worried he would sign up if the United States went to war. Eleanor had become fond of talkative, light-hearted Nick, and she went so far as to invite him to her grandmother's house in the country for a weekend. Her friends even decided that the two were secretly engaged, but her aunt wasn't convinced. When Bye organized a house party for Eleanor, she invited Nick only for the beginning of it and had Franklin come for the end. Eleanor wrote Franklin that her aunt thought it was better to have them "at different times!" She also told him she was sure her family thought her "either a dreadful flirt or an awfully poor one, I don't quite know which."

By late July 1904, when Franklin anchored the *Half Moon* in Dark Harbor, he had been hobbled for nearly eight months by his pledge of secrecy. As soon as he arrived, he sent a telegram to his mother telling her that he was fogged in, and then spent bright days walking and canoeing with Eleanor. When Franklin finally set sail for his family's summer house on Campobello Island, he pleaded with Eleanor to cut short her stay in Dark Harbor and visit him a few days earlier than she planned. She refused for lack of a chaperone.

That summer Eleanor was at ease with herself, and she had gained confidence in her ability to attract interesting men. But there was no question of her commitment. Summer pictures of Eleanor and Franklin are evocative and romantic. In almost all of them, Eleanor is wearing white, and she lifts her skirt and picks her way along the rocks toward Franklin, and they smile. In the way young children play, they push each other gently in their light summer clothes and duck their heads. In one sunny white group picture Franklin is standing possessively behind Eleanor, while she, seated, unaware, gazes demurely down.

"I wish you could have seen Franklin's face the night you left Campobello," a family friend wrote Eleanor. "He looked so tired and I felt everybody bored him."

Two months later, in October 1904, Eleanor and Franklin were still weeks away from announcing their engagement, but the secret was out. "Eleanor and Franklin are comic," Corinne Jr. wrote when they arrived in New Jersey for a house party. "They avoided each other like the black [plague] and told beautifully concocted lies and deceived in every direction." Franklin played the scene with such relish that Corinne Jr. told him he had a deceitful nature. A few days later, after a long, quiet drive with Eleanor when the other houseguests had left, she noted in her diary how nice it was to have Eleanor to herself. "Neither of us mentioned Franklin," she added, "but I think he was in both our minds."

In November, when the engagement was announced, Christine Roosevelt told Eleanor she was happy that her cousin would be staying in the family. She noted that Eleanor was the first and the youngest of the "Magic Five" to be engaged, and added, "I'm very jealous for I think Franklin is pretty nice, myself!" Other relatives were as pleased. Theodore wrote Franklin from the White House, "I am as fond of Eleanor as if she were my daughter; and I like you, and trust you, and believe in you." Corinne Jr. noted in her diary that Franklin was "a love," and that she was "thrilled" by his engagement to "darling Eleanor." Bye told Eleanor that he was exactly like his father, the "most *absolutely* honorable upright gentleman" she had ever known. Alice teased Eleanor that she was an "old fox" for having kept her engagement secret, and told her she would be delighted to be her maid of honor. But mentally Alice tapped her foot. Her long list of loves didn't make up for not having a fiancé herself.

1904 WAS A PRESIDENTIAL election year, and Theodore was forced to court the American people as circumspectly as Franklin had courted Eleanor, for custom dictated that a president couldn't "go on the stump" and couldn't "indulge in personalities." But Theodore had done the next best thing. The year before, comfortably in advance of the campaign season, he had made a leisurely goodwill tour through the West, cementing ties with old friends and wooing new voters. He had come home full of the West; finding the Grand Canyon "beautiful and terrible and unearthly," he had felt as if he were "gazing at a sunset of strange and awful splendor." He had also come home with additions to the family zoo: two bears, one horse, one lizard, a horned toad, and a badger, a typically Theodore variation on "The Twelve Days of Christmas."

Back in Washington, Theodore had felt "blank horror" because nothing required his attention. He had become frustrated in his physical pursuits as well, having given up his boxing lessons because he felt it hardly befitted a president to present himself in public with a black eye, particularly in an election year. He had continued to wrestle several times a week with two Japanese athletes, but three months before the Republican National Convention one of them choked him in a stranglehold, and it gave him pause. Quite possibly, forty-five-year-old Theodore admitted, he was no longer of an age or build "to be whirled lightly over an opponent's head."

Alice was trying to stay out of trouble, too, and her diary reads with nunlike simplicity. Entries noting sedate lunches with the children are interspersed with reports of "church with father" and "church with mother." She also wrote that she wished she could sleep through the year and wake up to find the election "victoriously, jubilantly, triumphantly over."

Although his Democratic opponent, the New York judge Alton B. Parker, seemed to present little threat, Theodore wrote to one of his sons that it was "utterly impossible to say what the outcome will be." As Election Day approached, he became convinced that something would go wrong. Finally it did. Two weeks before the election, Parker began to imply that, despite Theodore's anti-corporate stance, sizable business contributions were supporting the Republican campaign. Both Theodore and Alice feared the worst. "I am positive he won't be elected," she wrote in her diary on November 1, 1904. "It looks as if it were all drifting the other direction."

Five days before the election, on November 3, Parker accused George Cortelyou, the chairman of the Republican National Committee, of actually blackmailing corporations into making large contributions to the campaign. The next day, spurning all advice—and ignoring the stricture against indulging in personalities—Theodore declared Parker's charges "monstrous" and "slanderous." Afterward he wrote his son Kermit, "I never believe in hitting soft, I hit him in a way he will remember." Not until eight years later would it come out that the Republican National Committee, needing funds more than honor, had accepted the monies without telling Theodore.

In 1904, however, Theodore carried the day. His statement, made so close to the election, gave Parker no time to rally a defense. The voting on November 8, which everyone except Theodore and his daughter had always believed would be in his favor, indeed turned out to elect him in a landslide. The next afternoon Wilbur Wright took off from a cow pasture

Franklin joking with friends

Theodore touring the West in 1903

*Theodore on the
way to the Capitol on
Inauguration Day,
March 4, 1905*

*Ted (center), wounded
on the football field
at Harvard*

near Dayton, Ohio, and flew three miles—the longest flight to date—to celebrate what he called Theodore's phenomenal political victory. Like the president, Wright landed safely.

FOUR MONTHS LATER, on the night of March 4, 1905, the Roosevelt cousins and the rest of Washington made their way to the Pension Building on F Street for the Inaugural Ball. The Washington Monument appeared to be suspended in the evening sky—an effect achieved by placing searchlights on the roof of the Bureau of Engraving and Printing—and thousands of lights outlined the buildings on Pennsylvania Avenue.

Hours earlier, Theodore had stood before the crowd and delivered his brief, simply worded inaugural address. It was part of the image he was creating: that he was an average man like everyone else. The older and more famous Theodore grew, the more he tried to typify the ordinary. In a few years his autobiography would contain the same message: that he was just a regular fellow who had to work very hard.

Eleanor said later that she and Franklin were so busy watching Theodore, they didn't listen to his speech. But then she probably knew his simple words were meant for the public, designed to disguise a complex man. Years later, like him, she would deprecate herself in her autobiography, possibly in part because she, too, wanted to align herself with America's ordinary citizens. One of her biographers, James Kearney, theorized that Eleanor had written mostly about the unhappy times in her early life because she wished to associate herself with the "agonizing insecurity and aspirations of American youth in the thirties."

For Franklin, the inauguration reinforced the dream he had had since his sophomore year at Harvard that someday he would be elected president. His plans were beginning to crystallize. He would campaign for the New York State legislature, then get himself appointed assistant secretary of the Navy. After that he would run for governor. He would tell a friend in a few months that "anyone with a little luck who was elected the governor of New York had a good chance of winning the presidency." It happened to be the same path Theodore had taken to the White House, and years later Eleanor said that Franklin had been influenced in his decision to enter politics "partly by the glamour" of his cousin's example. When Franklin did achieve public office, his personality was often contrasted with his cousin's. Those who believed Theodore had been guileless and straightforward described Franklin as manipulative and devious. But at least one biography of Theodore—which Edith claimed she could not put down—disagreed. Lewis Einstein, the biographer who she believed best understood her husband, described Theodore as "subtle, intricate, and elusive," three adjectives usually applied to Franklin.

Seventeen-year-old Ted stayed close to his father that day. Theodore had assumed the presidency as the result of an assassination, and his oldest son was known in the family for his laconic bravery. After a football game, Ted mentioned to his mother as an afterthought that he had broken his nose. He dreamed of becoming a soldier, but his father thought men who spent their lives in the military lacked ambition. Theodore told Ted that he could win a "greater prize" in civilian life.

On the reviewing stand that afternoon, Alice—"in white voile dress & huge black hat," her cousin Corinne Jr. noted in her diary—had been out of sorts. Her father had jumped up so many times to wave at his constituents that one newspaper wrote he looked just like the jack-in-the-box replicas of him being sold as souvenirs along Pennsylvania Avenue. Alice had waved, too, but her father had told her to stop.

"Well, you do it," she said. "Why shouldn't I?"

"But this is *my* inauguration," Theodore answered.

Later Alice said that it galled her to hear her father, "one of the greatest experts in publicity there ever was, accusing me of trying to steal his limelight."

As if anyone could. At the Inaugural Ball, an electrician threw a lever and sixty thousand tiny lights twinkled in the rotunda of the Pension

Building. They illuminated the caves with lichen-covered rocks and the waterfalls and aquatic plants that had been imported to transform the huge room into an exotic party scene. In the middle of the splendor, framed by the starry firmament, average and unassuming Theodore waved at the crowd "to deafening applause."

Roosevelt Weds Roosevelt

THEODORE BROUGHT his high-voltage limelight along with him two weeks later when he drew up to the Parish-Ludlow residence at 6–8 East 76th Street in the green tumult of St. Patrick's Day. Wherever he went, no matter what the event, Theodore was the star attraction. It suited him perfectly. As Alice said, her father liked to be "the bride at every wedding and the corpse at every funeral." On March 17, 1905, Eleanor, upstairs in her wedding dress, listened to the crowds outside cheer top-hatted Theodore, a bunch of wilted shamrocks in his lapel. The streets were so clogged with his admirers and the seventy-five policemen dispatched to protect him that latecomers were unable to get to the house.

"Only think of Franklin," Pussie prescribed in a note delivered to Eleanor's room while she waited. "Drink a cup of strong tea half an hour before you go down stairs. *No* sugar or cream in it. It will give you color & make you feel well." It was the sort of note a mother, conscious of her daughter's fatigue and consequent pallor, anxious that she would appear at her best, might have written.

Her aunt's brief maternal rush aside, Eleanor's unprotected state was evident on her wedding day. In 1905, a daughter's marriage symbolized the continuation of tradition, and the ceremony attested to her family's dignity and pride. But at Eleanor's wedding there was neither a proud father nor a loving mother present. Reporting on her marriage, one newspaper referred to her bluntly as "an orphan." The ceremony took place in her cousin Susie's house, and the reception was given by her grandmother. A few guests complained of the second-rate food and the uninspired flower arrangements, and a reporter commented on the narrow and ungenerous staircase that allowed only one bridesmaid to descend at a time.

Those things meant little to the Roosevelt family. They knew their ties would be strengthened by Eleanor and Franklin's marriage. At 3:30, the first bridesmaids, Alice and Corinne Jr., walked side by side in long white silk gowns trimmed in lace and silver; three silver-tipped feathers, reminiscent of the Roosevelt crest, secured their hair. The girls were confident that the ceremony would consecrate a happy marriage. Alice told an interviewer years later that she thought Franklin had been "very much in love with Eleanor when he married her," and Corinne Jr. wrote in her diary that she was sure they would have a "wonderfully congenial" life together.

In the double drawing room, made by sliding open the doors between the Parish and Ludlow houses, the decorations might not have been lavish in the eyes of some, but the yellow-brocaded walls were twined with clematis, and they glowed in the candlelight. Hundreds of pink roses made an arch in front of the large mantel on the west side of the room. The Hyde Park Roosevelts and the Oyster Bay Roosevelts watched approvingly as the rest of the bridesmaids—Helen Cutting, Isabella Selmes, Muriel Delano Robbins, and Ellen Delano, carrying large bouquets of pink roses—made their way to the altar. They were followed by Theodore, on whose arm was Eleanor, the daughter of his dead brother.

Years earlier, Edith had predicted that her niece, the ugly duckling, might turn into a swan, and that day, in the opinion of at least one newspaper, Eleanor had "more claim to good looks than any of the Roosevelts." As Nick Biddle and the other ushers held the lengths of white satin ribbon that made a wedding aisle, Eleanor, tall and straight-backed, holding delicate lilies of the valley, walked past men who loved her.

Because Nick had had his own thoughts about wanting to marry

Eleanor and Franklin in Hyde Park in 1905

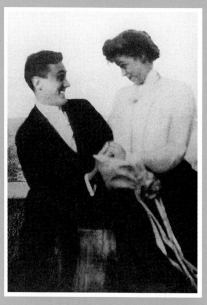

*Franklin and Eleanor teasing each other
in Newburgh, New York, in 1905*

Eleanor in her wedding dress on March 17, 1905

*Eleanor with the first baby, Anna; Franklin;
and their dog, Duffy, at Campobello in 1907*

Eleanor, he had tried and failed three times before he finally succeeded in composing a note of congratulations to Franklin. Another usher, Howard Cary, commented ruefully on how uncomfortable Eleanor must have been in Dark Harbor when he kept asking her to tea and dinner and to take walks along the ocean while all the time she had been engaged. Howard's mother had said, a bit sadly, to Eleanor, "So you are not going to be my daughter-in-law after all." Lyman Delano called his cousin Franklin the luckiest of men, and Laura Delano knew her brother meant it; years later she recalled that she had watched him fall "very much in love with Eleanor." According to friends, several other men, including Duncan Harris, Harry Hooker, and Robert Ferguson, were to be counted among the bride's admirers. Laura Delano said that Eleanor had those men "under her thumb. They would fall at her feet." But Eleanor had not hesitated to say yes when Franklin told her that he loved her and asked her to marry him. "I knew that I loved him, too," she later wrote. "I was happiest when I was with him." When Eleanor reached the altar, she handed Alice her bouquet and took her place beside the groom.

Franklin would always mask his deepest emotions (in his diary he used a secret code to write that Eleanor was an angel), but in an interview he once revealed why he had fallen in love with Eleanor. She had a quality "every member of the Roosevelt family seems always to have had," he said: "a deep and abiding interest in everything and everyone." And in a novel Franklin began after they were married, he wrote, "If there is anything in the theory that husband and wife should be as different as possible from each other, the Richards disproved it, for Mrs. Richards was in a thousand ways a female counterpart of her husband." Franklin and Eleanor were each drawn to the Rooseveltness of the other, to a shared family style that was generations old, for the common genealogical spring that nourished them both had not shifted course in more than two hundred years. "Franklin calm and happy," Sara wrote in her diary on March 17. "Eleanor the same."

After the ceremony, at which the Rev. Endicott Peabody officiated, Theodore said, "Well, Franklin, there's nothing like keeping the name in the family." Then the president strode off to find the refreshments—"only a fleeting glimpse of a bottle of champagne," one man complained—and most of the admiring guests abandoned Eleanor and Franklin briefly to follow him. The friends and relatives who stayed behind were greeted by the bride, wearing, as her mother and grandmother had before her, a length of priceless Brussels lace, kept in a vault between weddings. Her neck was fragile in a collar of pearls, and her heavy ivory gown swung slowly around her slender body as she turned first to one relative's kiss and then another's.

Of the "Magic Five" cousins, Elfrida would marry a few months later, in June 1905; Dorothy married in 1907; and Christine followed in 1909. They appeared briefly in the newspapers at the time of their weddings before returning to the privacy of quiet lives, as they had once played on a darkening lawn until they were lost to view. Eleanor was different from these cousins. The Roosevelt qualities of curiosity and interest were heightened in her, as they were in Franklin. They encourage forward movement, and so inclined her to a more vivid and public future.

Eleanor and Franklin left the reception, smiling and waving goodbye. They had cared enough to outwait Sara, and they were at ease with each other. That night, Alice wrote in her diary that she had gotten the ring favor in the wedding cake, which meant she was to be the next one to marry. She had already confessed that the idea of marriage appealed to her because she had a "decidedly animal streak." Back home in Oyster Bay, Theodore took a carriage ride with Edith down a country lane, where he halted his horse and embraced his wife of twenty years to the amusement of the children who were passing by. Passion seemed to be another part of the Roosevelt legacy.

Alice Rising

"THE EYES OF THE WORLD are upon her," one newspaper wrote. "It is a little trying," reported another slyly, "to keep a focus on Oyster Bay [where Theodore was] and on Manila [where Alice was] at the same time." Between them, the president and his twenty-one-year-old daughter earned yards of column space in the summer of 1905.

On February 8, 1904, a Japanese attack on the Russian fleet had signaled the beginning of the Russo-Japanese War; more than a year later, in a battle in the Korea Strait May 27–29, 1905, the Japanese had annihilated Russia as a naval power. Despite Theodore's contempt for the Russians, whose pogroms had killed many Jews, he wanted to help divide up the chips in the Far East in a way that would discourage any country's further attempts at world domination.

During the summer of 1905, while Theodore worked to negotiate a peace treaty between Russia and Japan, Alice checkered the Far East as if it were a game board. She landed in Hawaii on July 13, Japan on July 24, Manila on August 5, and Hong Kong on September 2. Why the president had dispatched his wayward young daughter on a trip through Asia at a critical moment in the peace talks seemed puzzling only at first. Alice might be inconsistent, but she had behaved herself in Puerto Rico two years before.

And she attracted attention wherever she went. Theodore knew that European royalty were free to tour the world, whereas tradition confined U.S. presidents to domestic travel. "Princess Alice," however, could go wherever he wished. His daughter's presence in any country would indicate his regard for it, but particularly in the Far East, where enormous value was placed on the family. What greater gesture of trust and respect for an Asian nation than for a world leader to send his daughter as his personal envoy? Theodore was betting that, because of Alice's visit, his peacemaking efforts would go more smoothly and his demands would gain wider public support in the Far East.

Had Theodore seen Alice's diary, it is doubtful he would have let her go. For months her entries had referred to "my Nick," and standing beside her as the ship left port in San Francisco was Ohio Congressman Nicholas Longworth. He was part of the seventy-five-member Far East delegation, led by Secretary of War William Howard Taft, that included congressmen, senators, Alice, and her chaperones. Nick was thirty-six, nearly bald, and not handsome, but he was popular with men and women alike. In a day when young men were expected to keep a proper distance, he didn't. It wasn't unusual for Alice to write of a dinner party, "Nick and I in a dark corner afterwards. It was quite wonderful." But she was just as likely to fret, "I know he doesn't *really* honestly care for poor little me," for she worried that Nick was unfaithful to her. Now, sailing to the Far East, she had him to herself.

Originally, the trip had been conceived of as a fact-finding mission, but it quickly developed feints and subplots. Privately, Theodore instructed Secretary Taft to find ways to tempt the Japanese to the peace table. Secrecy was critical, because any sort of large-scale deal-making required the approval of the Senate. The intrigue suddenly made the three-hundred-pound secretary of war seem like a shy suitor. He told newsmen that when he arrived in Japan, he would just "call at the Imperial Palace and leave his card." No one thought to ask him why he was traveling half the world to see a country in which he professed such casual interest.

The group aboard the Pacific Mail ship *Manchuria* reached Yokohama on July 24. All the way to Tokyo and an audience with the emperor, Alice saw roads lined with people bowing deeply in their honor. Enchanted, she grasped the arm of Lloyd Griscom, the U.S. ambassador to Japan. Even Taft, a seasoned politician, said he had never seen such crowds, and one American newspaper began to refer to the trip as "Alice Roosevelt's triumphal tour of the world." The tone of the Japanese press toward the American visitors was "absolutely unprecedented in warmth and friendliness." They called Alice the Princess Royal of America, and one Japanese newspaper told its readers that she often helped the president on missions where "tact and diplomacy" were necessary.

Reporters were impressed by Alice's dignity, but it was her natural- ness that charmed. When a young girl commented on how tiresome it must be to stand for hours shaking people's hands, Alice turned a shining face to her. "Tired?" she said. "Why I could throw my arms around their necks and kiss them!" Half a century later, Alice still took delight in recounting the antic moments of her Far East trip. She described, for an interviewer, an American Embassy garden party at which Japanese women had appeared carrying oriental parasols while also wearing wide- brimmed European hats. Alice chortled that they—and she—had looked as if they were in a "slightly stoned version" of the Ascot scene from *My Fair Lady.*

Quite naturally, the emperor of Japan sought to influence the progress of the peace negotiations through his treatment of the American president's daughter. At a formal dinner in her honor on July 26, Japanese Prime Minister Katsura raised his glass to Alice and said the banquet was evidence of his country's respect for her father. Three days later, Taft sent Theodore a cable confirming that his secret conversations had succeeded in securing from the Japanese the conditions under which they would end the war. Among them, Taft had agreed—with Theodore's prior approval— not to interfere with the Japanese occupation of Korea.

New York Herald Tribune

William Taft, center, with Alice at his feet and Nick Longworth to her right

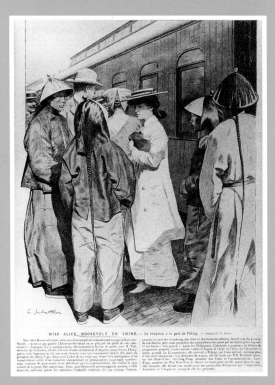

MISS ALICE ROOSEVELT EN CHINE. — Sa réception à la gare de Péking. — *Photographié M. Berger*

*Alice on her trip to China, as depicted
in a French newspaper*

*Alice Roosevelt and Nick Longworth,
leaning on the rail of the* Manchuria *as it
entered Manila harbor in 1905*

BACK HOME, the president was entertaining envoys from Russia and Japan at Sagamore Hill. He decided to invite them aboard the U.S.S. *Mayflower,* anchored in Oyster Bay. Amid the pomp, Theodore remained deliberately himself. He dodged the delicate protocol of order in entering the ship's dining room by saying, "Gentlemen, shall we go into luncheon?" Back at the house that evening around eleven, Theodore put out the dog and started shutting the windows, asking the Japanese diplomat Baron Kentaro Kaneko to wait while he closed up. Kaneko wondered where else in the world would a president show a foreign visitor to his room, carrying a candle to light the way and tossing an extra blanket on his guest's bed.

Despite everything, the peace talks foundered. The Japanese had been satisfied with annexing Korea, but now they also wanted Sakhalin, an island off the coast of Siberia. Russia wanted to retain possession of it. Theodore suggested through his emissaries that Sakhalin be divided between them. To nearly everyone's surprise, the Japanese government accepted the offer on August 29, and agreed to other concessions as well, among them, not requiring Russia to reimburse them for their costs in the war. Henry Adams complimented Theodore: "You have established a record as the best herder of emperors since Napoleon."

Meanwhile, on their honeymoon in Europe, Franklin and Eleanor were treated nearly as royally as Alice. While newspaper headlines praised the president's successful negotiations, hotel keepers hurried to cosset his young relatives in their finest rooms. "Everyone is talking about Cousin Theodore," Franklin wrote his mother from London. No one doubted that the president would be awarded the Nobel Prize for peace, the first to be given an American.

With the treaty agreed to, a holiday atmosphere took over aboard the *Manchuria.* One day Alice asked Lloyd Griscom whether in his opinion Nick was attractive. "Why, Alice, you couldn't find anybody nicer," Griscom replied. "I know, I know," she said, turning away. "But this is a question of marriage." The more cautious Taft became unnerved by the implications of seeing Alice and Nick breakfasting together every day and cavorting on deck. Gathering his courage, he asked Alice if they were engaged. "More or less, Mr. Secretary," she said cheerfully. "More or less."

The happy mood was short-lived. The people of Asia were disturbed when the terms of the peace treaty became known. The Japanese were appalled by the extent of their government's concessions. They did not want to share Sakhalin, and they wanted Russia to pay them back for what it had cost them to wage the war. Theodore moved quickly. He shuttled Alice around Asia in yet another monthlong goodwill tour. Alice had been shaking hands patiently and smiling for months. Now she had to take on new and delicate missions to China, Korea, and Japan without Secretary Taft, who had sailed for home. She entertained high-ranking officials so often in China that she complained she had no chance to sightsee.

But at the last stop, Alice didn't have to entertain. In Japan, hostility toward the United States had become so strong that when she and the others arrived in Tokyo on September 28, they were told that if any one of them found himself separated from the group, he should say he was English. When Alice finally landed back in the United States a month later, she showed considerable diplomatic discretion, telling reporters gathered on the pier in San Francisco that "not a single disagreeable incident marred our pleasure." Theodore allowed that his daughter had behaved "mighty well under rather trying circumstances."

The reporters wrote that they found Alice "characteristically quick and decisive" as she told the porters where to put her trunks. But at least one newsman sensed that something was different. Seeing Alice and Nick standing together, he asked the couple if they were engaged, but they only laughed.

The newsman was right, although Alice hesitated to tell her parents of her wish to marry a man so much older than herself. Finally, Alice blurted it out to Edith while she was brushing her teeth, so her stepmother could not instantly disapprove. But the fifteen-year age difference went unremarked, and Nick was welcomed into the family.

Four months later, on February 17, 1906, men in frock coats whizzed

Alice's trousseau,
illustrated in an
English newspaper

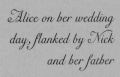

Alice on her wedding
day, flanked by Nick
and her father

COPYRIGHTED BY CURTIS 1906.

around the East Room of the White House clutching tripods. It was the morning of Alice's wedding. One photographer, carrying his heavy wooden equipment, slipped on the buffed and gleaming floor, slid into another photographer, then bumped into a third, who, lunging to protect his falling camera, slammed into everyone else.

When the gates to the White House finally opened, the wedding guests faced tight security. The police waited while Vice President Charles W. Fairbanks patted his pockets for his admittance card. Even Theodore's "doorkeeper," Major Loeffler, returning from an errand, was not allowed through for lack of a card. "But I must get in," he protested with the Alice in Wonderland logic that suited the day. "I am Major Loeffler." Franklin, who had his card, was one of the first through the gates. He was accompanied only by his mother, for Eleanor was expecting their first baby, and pregnant women rarely appeared in public.

Sara was undoubtedly pleased to have her son to herself for a day. She involved herself considerably with the young couple, arranging for them to move to 125 East 36th Street (where, in accordance with her daughter-in-law's wishes, there was a bedroom for Hall). She also insisted that Eleanor hire a nurse when Anna Eleanor was born, on May 3, 1906. Her daughter-in-law would acquiesce, although later, remembering her newborn—"by its mere helplessness winding itself inextricably around my heart"—Eleanor wished she had taken more care of the baby herself. But defying Sara was nearly unthinkable. In a year and a half, when Eleanor's second baby, James, was born and Franklin was a young lawyer at Carter, Ledyard and Millburn, her mother-in-law would plan a double town house for herself and her son's family at 47–49 East 65th Street. There, with its connecting doors, as in the Parish-Ludlow house, Sara would happen on the young couple "day or night." At least one guest, Margaret Cutter, sitting at tea with Eleanor, was unnerved by Sara's sudden appearance.

But for Alice on her wedding day, the tensions of marriage were still unknown and the air of antic joy continued. A gift in the form of two turtle doves, named Alice and Nick, were delivered in a wagon to the White House gate where sightseers clustered, hoping to catch a glimpse of the real-life couple when they left for their honeymoon. With four possible exit routes, the crowd was suggestible. They stationed themselves near the northwest gate, only to sweep off around a corner in pursuit of a rumor that a limousine belonging to Nick Longworth was parked at the west gate. Minutes later, a second getaway car, also owned by Nick, appeared at the southwest gate. Then a third car drew up to the front of the White House, facing north, while a fourth appeared at the east gate. No sooner did the crowd converge on that car than it sped off and parked behind the State Department Building. Two of the limousines honked in what onlookers took to be code, and members of the White House staff bustled outside to confer first with one chauffeur and then another. A newspaper said it seemed as if the entire intellectual strength of the administration had been enlisted to prevent anyone from learning which exit Alice and Nick would take.

Ever since the days when Theodore was the assistant secretary of the Navy, the country had been fascinated by Alice's highjinks. But now the much-talked-about willfulness of her girlhood had given way to the sense that a skittish Thoroughbred had been tamed, or had at least taken the first fence. That February, a newspaper told its readers that Alice's "desire for leadership" had been noticeable even when she was a child. She had always demanded the best place at the toy tea table for herself and her doll. Reporters said Alice had inherited her father's impulsive temperament and directness of action. In 1906 they found her a "well-read woman, a brilliant conversationalist and thoroughly familiar with affairs of public interest."

February 17 was a "brisk, kindly Winter day," one newspaper reported. Sunshine flooded the East Room as Alice, smiling easily and chatting with her father, her hand on his arm, walked down the aisle at noon past the eight hundred guests. Minutes later, Alice startled them when, in the middle of taking her vows, she glanced wistfully over at her stepmother. After the ceremony, she turned from Nick and embraced Edith. The two spoke quietly for a moment, then Alice kissed her father. Together with her excited younger brothers and sister, they made a pretty scene. Orange blossoms wreathed Alice's face, holding her veil in place, and were tucked decoratively into the buckles of her shoes. The neckline of her dress was edged in lace from her mother's wedding gown, and her twelve-foot satin train was embroidered with the Roosevelt coat of arms.

Alice appeared most truly Roosevelt in the moment she became Mrs. Longworth, but according to her, somewhere in that day, Edith told her she was glad to see her leave. Her stepdaughter had been nothing but trouble, she said. Alice knew she had been a difficult child. She also knew she had suffered painful rejections at her parent's hands. But apparently Edith's frustrations were released in that awful moment, for the air between them softened from then on. Alice later claimed that when Edith was very old she apologized for having been unkind to her when she was a girl. But by then Alice and her stepmother had been friends for years. There was no need then to reconcile in the present, and it was much too late to recover the past.

The entire nation celebrated Alice's wedding. In Boston, the birthplace of Alice's mother, and in nearby villages as well, the bells of the churches and the public buildings rang for fifteen minutes. In Pittsburgh, two thousand shop girls tied up traffic, crowding into the street and cheering when the bulletin came that Alice was married.

Back in Washington, the patient crowd waited and saw nothing. They did not notice the raised window in the back of the White House. Alice, dressed in almond-colored silk (later wondering why she had chosen such a dull color), ducked out of it with Nick. They climbed into the honeymoon car, which raced over from behind the State Department Building, and waved goodbye in a shower of rice. Theodore stood in the middle of the driveway and threw an old shoe after them as they drove away.

PART THREE

SHIFTING ALLIANCES

1910 – 1918

Two Cousins Campaign

BEFORE THE PRESIDENTIAL campaign of 1932, James Farley, the head of the Democratic National Committee, was asked who he thought might make a winning Democratic candidate. "Well," the chairman answered, "there's this fellow named Franklin Delano Roosevelt. . . . He's got a fine name—everybody remembers Teddy. He's also got a great smile and he's got a wonderful voice." Was that why Farley had decided Franklin would be a good presidential candidate? someone asked. "Yeah," said the chairman. "Great name, great voice, great smile."

But on a warm summer day in 1910, the chairman of New York state's Dutchess County Democratic Committee, Edward E. Perkins, was less impressed. Franklin had been summoned to a Poughkeepsie office by Democratic leaders in the counties that made up the twenty-sixth state senatorial district. Perkins appraised the bareheaded young man in jodhpur boots and riding breeches without enthusiasm, but he accepted Franklin as a candidate and said merely, "You'll have to take off those yellow shoes and put on some regular pants." He didn't think that Franklin could win the race for the state senate. No one did. In the previous fifty years the farmers had elected only one Democratic state senator, and the committeemen gave Franklin a 20 percent chance of being the second. State

Assemblyman Lewis Stuyvesant Chanler concluded, "You fellows don't need a candidate. You need a sucker."

Because the Democratic candidate for the twenty-sixth district couldn't hope to win, custom dictated that he enhance the party profile. Franklin, from a wealthy Democratic family, could do that, simply by making a few speeches in the principal towns in the district. Campaigning among the hidebound Republican farmers was considered a waste of everyone's time. Writing about Franklin's Republican opponent, one newspaper summed it up: "[Mr.] Schlosser, we imagine, will not be greatly disturbed by Mr. Roosevelt's candidacy."

But two Democrats, District Attorney John Mack and Poughkeepsie Mayor John K. Sague, who were in the room with County Chairman Ed Perkins when Franklin showed up, were pleased with his nomination. He represented the beginning of a statewide drive to attract progressive young candidates to the Democratic cause. The Democrats in the state's largest city, New York, were dominated by the Tammany machine, a long-established network of old-line party bosses who dispensed patronage and traded political favors. Reform politicians such as Mack and Sague were eager to loosen Tammany's hold on the party, and their strategy was to sign up young independent Democrats, the more the better.

Franklin took his nomination seriously and campaigned for four weeks in a rented red Maxwell touring car with no top and no windshield. Farmers disliked cars because they frightened their animals, but Franklin calculated that a horse and buggy would be too slow. If his driver averaged twenty-two miles per hour, the candidate and the Maxwell would have time to cover the two thousand miles of roads in the three counties—Putnam, Columbia, and Dutchess—that made up his district.

New York State law at the time required that when the driver of a car met a wagon or a carriage on the road, he had to pull over and shut off the engine. Franklin took the opportunity to do a little politicking with the other driver during these forced stops. As a child, he had held the reins of his father's horse while James talked comfortably with the country people in Hyde Park about crop failure and drought. Franklin's charm—what at least one journalist has referred to as the "ur-attribute" of every successful politician, the attribute without which every other quality is useless—sprang, like his father's, from his interest in how people led their lives. A Hyde Park man saw Franklin as a natural politician because of the way he treated the people he met: "He would approach them as a friend . . . with that smile of his—would lead up to the fact that he was a candidate for the senatorship."

Campaigning meant that Franklin drove on back roads rutted with carriage tracks and put up with the wind and rain that came across the Maxwell's hood. He had to limp painfully in and out of the car after being knocked off a trolley by an ice wagon. But he persevered, and stopped the Maxwell wherever he saw workmen in the fields, or trains he could meet, or a chance to stand drinks in local bars. Franklin's opponents derided the bunting-draped Maxwell and called his experiment a "vaudeville tour," but he averaged eight to ten speeches and thirty miles a day.

Despite his inexperience and the difficulties, Franklin was always enthusiastic. More important, according to his law partner Langdon Marvin, he was "anxious to do the right thing. . . . Especially, I believe he wanted to do 'the right thing.'" Many years later, Eleanor said she doubted that Franklin had ever worked harder in his life. For although he had the makings of a natural politician, he was not a seasoned public speaker. Eleanor remembered he spoke so slowly that "there would be a long pause, and I would be worried for fear he would never go on."

Margaret Richardson, who would soon marry Hall, spent considerable time in the Roosevelt household. Although Eleanor had just given birth to a baby, Elliott, on September 23, 1910, Margaret remembered that she was caught up in Franklin's first race and worked "very hard" in it.

I N 1910, when Franklin was campaigning, his cousin was no longer president. By 1908, Theodore had served nearly two terms—the balance of McKinley's second and one of his own. Tradition had it that presidents

The Roosevelt family at Christmas, 1908,
shortly before leaving the White House. From left:
Ethel, Ted, Quentin, Edith, Theodore, Kermit,
Archie, Alice, and Nick

Alice, pictured with her brother Kermit in 1909,
drew closer to her family after her marriage.

Franklin giving a speech in Dutchess County in 1910

never served more than twice, and Theodore felt that for him to run again would violate the spirit of the unwritten law; if he won, he would occupy the White House for eleven unbroken years. Instead, he had backed his good friend and former cabinet member William Howard Taft. When Taft won the presidency, Theodore sailed to Africa for a year of big-game hunting.

When he returned home from his safari, he came by way of Europe. NOT TO BE SHOT, a *Punch* cartoon cautioned him, pointing to the lions in Trafalgar Square. King Edward VII had died just before Theodore reached London, and the former president enjoyed the contrast between his plain black coat and the robes and crowns of the nine European monarchs present at the funeral. He was amused to see that the kings bowed less attentively over the coffin than they did over him. As one observer put it, "The kings have been fairly scrambling for a share in his conversation."

Alice joined her father in London. He thought she had settled down nicely since her marriage and was an asset to Nick. She was useful to Theodore as well. In London, Alice said, they stayed up "late into the night" in her room discussing the political scene in America. Theodore was interested to hear more about the way the commitment to fight bossism was cutting across party lines. Progressives in both parties were on the rise and calling for a wide variety of changes in the political system. Theodore counted himself among the nation's most outspoken advocates of reform, and when he returned to the United States, he used the New York State Republican convention to call for a series of progressive measures. He didn't run for office himself in 1910, but campaigned aggressively for many of the progressive Republican candidates.

That autumn, the seasoned Republican Theodore Roosevelt and his young Democratic cousin were joined in the battle to reform New York. The sight fascinated Republicans and Democrats alike, and the newspapers were charmed. They wrote that Franklin had the "finely chiseled face of a Roman patrician," but that "nature has left much unfinished in modeling the face of the Roosevelt of greater fame." Republican Party members wanted Theodore to speak out against Franklin, but he refused. Although his father, Theodore Sr., had switched to the Republican ticket during the Civil War, Roosevelts had often been Democrats.

It seemed only natural for Franklin to follow his father, James, into the Democratic Party, but in fact he had weighed the decision carefully. Theodore had "infected" many Roosevelt cousins "with large ambitions as citizens," as the cousins' aunt Ella Bulloch pointed out. She marveled at their growing number, with "Uncle Ted in the extraordinary position of being the arbiter of the Republican destinies." Newsmen referred to Theodore's eldest son, Ted, as "the Crown Prince," because they expected him to enter politics, and Helen's husband, Teddy Robinson, planned to campaign for a Republican seat in the New York State Assembly. Soon young Corinne Jr.'s husband, Joseph Alsop, would run as a Republican for state office in Connecticut; she would follow him in 1924. Franklin told his friend Alice Sohier that Republicans aplenty were growing up around Theodore. He would be a Democrat partly in order to distinguish himself from them.

That these male cousins were Franklin's potential rivals did not affect his fondness for them. He and Teddy Robinson liked to hunt, and since their wives were close friends, they saw each other regularly at house parties, dinners, and dances. Joe Alsop and Corinne Jr. sometimes joined the two couples in Hyde Park for ice-skating and baseball games, and on New Year's Eve the group went to the Rogerses' annual party together. For years the cousins formed a major part of Eleanor and Franklin's social life.

Nicholas Longworth, Alice's conservative Republican husband, was running for congressional office in 1910. Alice brightened the Ohio Grange halls of his campaigns, and she made it a rule, at the end of a meeting, to shake as many hands as he did. But it was the last time for some years that she would publicly support Nick's career. He and Theodore pushed from opposite ends of the Republican seesaw, and her support for one would only point up her failure to help the other.

To everyone's surprise, Franklin captured his state senate seat handily—with a majority of 1,140 votes. Immediately, he and Eleanor made plans to move to Albany. Most young state senators and assemblymen lived in boardinghouses when they first came to the small political capital, but Franklin could afford to rent a house, and he wanted his family with him.

In New York City, in their double town house, Eleanor had been reluctant to challenge her mother-in-law, and she had worked hard to keep relations within the family tranquil. But peace came at a high price. Sara often told Eleanor's children, "I am more your mother than your mother is. Your mother only bore you." She was, as the oldest boy, James, put it later, "in constant competition with Mother." But in Albany, in the brownstone at 248 State Street, Eleanor was free. She hired the staff she wanted, spent her afternoons with the children, and stepped, wide-eyed, into public life with her young husband. For although the reporter Louis Howe believed a first-time state senator ranked "somewhere between . . . a janitor and a committee clerk," Franklin became a widely known politician before he ever voted on a bill.

In those days, a candidate for the United States Senate was selected at a caucus of state senators and assemblymen. Everyone who attended his party's decision-making meeting was honor-bound to vote for the candidate chosen. Before the 1911 Democratic caucus, word went out that the choice for U.S. senator would be a Tammany Hall favorite, William F. Sheehan. To the proponents of reform, his selection would represent a step backward.

Many Democrats in the state senate and assembly didn't want to have to vote for "Blue-eyed Billy." Franklin spent hours walking through the streets of Albany, trying to decide what he should do, and finally he spoke with a dissenter, Edmund Terry. Together they spread the word that they would not attend the caucus. Instead, they encouraged the other dissenters to gather with them at the Ten Eyck Hotel. Terry calculated that if eighteen men refused to attend the caucus, they would be able to join with the Republicans and block Sheehan. The meeting began at nine o'clock on the evening of January 16, 1911, and "for ten long minutes that seemed like hours," Terry remembered, he and Franklin waited in the Ten Eyck Hotel.

They kept assuring each other of the imminent "speedy arrival" of their colleagues. To their relief, they came. Eventually, twenty-one Democrats would refuse to vote for Sheehan.

Franklin, Terry, and the other "insurgents" represented various interests, which made the group difficult to organize. The one issue they agreed on was their repudiation of bossism, but that just made them suspicious of any leader. Franklin was the only state senator to sign the initial draft of a "statement of principles." Because they lacked cohesion, Franklin thought the group would be less vulnerable to outside pressure if they were gathered together physically. So every morning at ten o'clock, they assembled in Eleanor and Franklin's library and walked to the statehouse. When the session was over, they spent the rest of the day and evening in the Roosevelt house, trading political gossip and plotting ways to topple Sheehan. Louis Howe wrote that the mutiny was "led by a 'new senator' without experience in the game, who looks like a boy."

Regular Democratic faithfuls accused the insurgents of betrayal. Sheehan told Franklin that their action against him was assassination; the dissenters were pressured on all sides, their political careers threatened. Eleanor later wrote that the possibility of reprisals had angered her so much her "blood boiled." Frances Perkins, who would be one of Franklin's longtime colleagues, remembered that "they told him that it was going to ruin him." But behind Franklin's "highly polished exterior," wrote the *New York Times,* lay "quiet force and determination," and he held the group together. "During the time when we were hounded and harassed," Terry recalled, "he was the shepherd of the flock." Louis Howe had a different rural descriptive: "The donkey's got his ears back." But most Tammany regulars just thought Franklin was making "an ass of himself."

After two months, the dissenters finally succeeded in stonewalling the selection of Sheehan, though Tammany Hall wasn't about to be bested by a group of reformists. Eventually James A. O'Gorman, another candidate who suited the leaders of the political machine, was selected. But Franklin had proved himself in his battle against Sheehan. "Just a line to

Alice and Nick traveled often between Rookwood, the Longworth family home in Ohio, and Washington, D.C.

Eleanor as a young mother in 1909

Albany, New York State's capital, in the early 1900s

From the first, Sara was a constant, domineering presence in Eleanor and Franklin's life together.

say we are all really proud of the way you handled yourself," Theodore wrote him.

Franklin's dramatic entry into New York state politics reminded people of his cousin's attitude as state assemblyman years before. Theodore, too, had refused to bow to the pressure of a Democratic political machine so deeply entrenched that its power extended to Republicans as well. One political leader, remembering Theodore's early resistance to Tammany Hall, suggested that they should drown his cousin Franklin while he was still young. "That Franklin Roosevelt is faster than T.R. ever was," an observer noted in 1911. "His seat wasn't warm before he became a bolter."

Eleanor later claimed that the arguments about Sheehan had been of little interest to her. But nearly every day for months, she and Franklin made their home available to politicians and she got to know them, she herself wrote, "very well." Franklin thought his wife's "political sagacity" began that year, and Margaret Richardson remembered that she attended "all the sessions of the Senate" and "sat up all night listening to the debates." When Eleanor and Franklin were apart, his letters outlined points of legislation with an attention to detail that assumed her knowledge and interest. "Well of course I told Franklin I didn't agree with that," Margaret remembered her saying. "Franklin knows I don't approve of this." Nonpartisan by nature, Eleanor was attracted to anyone interested in reform, even Tammany loyalists, and her friendships helped smooth the way for Franklin's later dealings with them. Langdon Marvin remembered that "everyone in Albany loved her."

At twenty-six Eleanor was an appealing woman. Her hair, wound thickly on her head, emphasized her slender neck, and her slim figure was suited to the narrow elegance of the dresses and long fur scarves that Franklin had bought her in Paris on their honeymoon. As a mother of three, she seemed to take things in stride. Jennie Delano had been sure her cousin-by-marriage would be a wonderful mother from the "natural way in which she accepts everything." In 1911, Eleanor's daughter, Anna, was five, James three and a half, and Elliott just a baby. Only her twenty-year-old brother, Hall, a frequent presence in the household, was cause for worry.

Though a brilliant student at Harvard, he was probably showing signs of the heavy drinking that would one day destroy his liver and end his life. Hall was reckless and charming, and Eleanor later told a friend sadly that she had known from the time he was eighteen that "the only way that anyone could hold him was to let him go."

Eleanor's interest in "everything and everyone" remained undiminished despite her concern about Hall and her busy household. She would write of those years that something in her had "craved to be an individual," but it was clear she had already become one. In Hyde Park, Eleanor's distinctive, gentle presence was a welcome contrast to Sara's domineering ways: Helen, who often stayed in her father's house next door, had been strongly tempted not to comply when Sara once demanded that she meet her in New York after a European trip.

Everyone looked forward to Eleanor and Franklin's holiday visits to Hyde Park. At Christmastime, Franklin read aloud Charles Dickens's *A Christmas Carol,* and he adopted a different voice for each character—a whisper for one, a guttural rasp for another, and a high, piping cry for Tiny Tim. On Christmas morning, after the children opened their stockings, he took them sledding. Toward dusk, as always, Franklin lighted the candles he had placed on the tree, and the family gathered to open their presents.

Guests often joined them, and were astonished by the number of gifts they received from Eleanor. "Everyone had a chair with presents. Big boxes and small boxes and tiny little things, you know," said one awed young recipient. "Full of surprises. Maybe twenty presents!" Franklin basked in his wife's generosity. Usually it took him days to open all of his gifts, because he refused to put one down until he had savored it fully, a habit that led Eleanor to declare that the "nicest men" kept the qualities of small boys when they were grown.

Early in the new year, politicians began to prepare for the 1912 presidential campaign. Letters poured into Sagamore Hill urging Theodore to run again. But he had been out of office for a term, and the prospect appeared to hold little appeal. "They have no business to expect me to take command of a ship simply because the ship is sinking" was his response.

Nevertheless, the noncandidate did set off on a speaking tour of sixteen states, and twenty-five reporters went along with him. Privately, Theodore was struck by the strength of the movement behind the Republican senator Robert La Follette, who for ten years had been calling for a variety of progressive measures. Political observers were sure the Wisconsin legislator would decide to run for president. Theodore bought time to make his own decision: He encouraged Republican state groups to send progressive delegates to the national convention uncommitted to a specific candidate. By calling for uncommitted Republican delegations, he was able to foster the progressive movement without promoting La Follette. The tactic also left the delegates free to vote for Theodore if he chose to run.

After several months of constantly reassessing the strength of the progressive Republican delegates, Theodore became convinced that he could win the presidential nomination. On February 21, 1912, he declared his candidacy, announcing that his hat was in the ring. Embellishing the boxing term with his own particular enthusiasm, he added, "The fight is on and I am stripped to the buff."

The Republican Party immediately rose up. Not only was Theodore trying to usurp La Follette's progressive power base, but he was also opposing his former protégé, the incumbent president, William Howard Taft. Alice was suddenly at her father's side. "I think she felt she just had to see me," Theodore wrote Kermit, "because of course all respectable society is now apoplectic with rage over me."

Divided Loyalties

THE FUTURES OF the Roosevelt cousins were tied in conflicting ways to the outcome of the 1912 Democratic National Convention at the Fifth Regiment Armory in Baltimore. Franklin was trying to cajole, joke, or argue the delegates into nominating New Jersey's progressive governor, Woodrow Wilson, for president. Alice and her brother Kermit, who joined Eleanor and Franklin at the convention, hoped—for the sake of their father's presidential chances—that Wilson would lose.

Eleanor found her Oyster Bay cousins "restless and unhappy." Kermit told Franklin that his father was "praying" for the more conservative Democrat, Champ Clark, to win the presidential nomination. If Clark became the party's candidate, progressive Democrats across the country would vote for Theodore.

The convention proceedings dragged as the chairman kept polling and repolling the delegates, hypnotizing spectator and delegate alike. At four in the morning, newsmen found society women in their long gloves still "sticking to their posts like patriots." On the fourth day, June 29, Tammany Hall boss Charles F. Murphy broke the stalemate by casting New York State's ninety votes for Clark. Alice and Kermit were elated, but a leading Democratic progressive, Nebraskan delegate William Jennings

Bryan, was alarmed. Murphy's vote had suddenly put Clark ahead, and Bryan leaped to his feet. "As long as New York's vote is recorded for Mr. Clark," he stated, "I withhold my vote for him and cast it—" In the ensuing uproar, no one heard the name, but everyone knew it. Woodrow Wilson had catapulted to national prominence the year before. From the day in January 1911 when Wilson was sworn into office as the governor of New Jersey, he had begun pushing through reforms. His state had become among the most progressive in the country.

But despite Champ Clark's lead, Alice and Kermit were worried. Bryan's support had greatly strengthened Wilson's position. They knew, because of the events at the Republican convention the week before, that their father sorely needed the Democratic Party's progressive vote.

Theodore had arrived in Chicago on June 15 for the Republican convention with nearly a majority of the delegates already committed to him. He had won them by going directly to the people in the primary campaign. Seemingly, he was in an excellent position to secure the votes necessary for nomination. But Theodore knew that at the national convention his Republican opponent, President Taft, as the incumbent, would dominate. He also knew that many delegate seats were contested, claimed by both Taft and him. So Theodore, planning ahead, had decided to try the unthinkable: He would launch a third political party if the Republican National Committee threw out the delegates he considered rightfully his and put Taft's in their place.

Many of Theodore's longtime advisors had fallen away in this run for the presidency. Increasingly, he turned to his eldest daughter. Initially, Alice had opposed her father's candidacy, because she knew that President Taft would ultimately broker the proceedings. But at the same time, she could not believe that the additional delegates won by her father at the convention would be taken from him. Gradually, she allowed herself to hope that he would be nominated.

Alice never forgot the "savage excitement" of the hours on June 18 before the Republican convention opened. Her brother Ted went from room to room in Chicago's Congress Hotel assessing the number of

Theodore's delegates, while a newspaper assessed him: "The heir of Theodore Rex has none of the assertiveness of his papa nor of his half-sister Alice." Alice and Edith retreated from the bedlam to shorten the speech Theodore planned to give. By contrast, young Nicholas Roosevelt, assigned to keep an eye on Taft headquarters, claimed to find it so quiet that "Roosevelt men" went there when they needed to rest.

Nevertheless, when the Republican convention came to order, in state after state men loyal to Taft overcame Theodore's delegates. The constant roar from Roosevelt supporters was "Thou shalt not steal!" But it was to no avail, and Taft won the nomination. Alice followed her father out of the convention and over to Orchestra Hall on Michigan Avenue, where the delegates who had refused to vote for Taft had gathered. Three hundred forty-four people ripped off their Republican badges and acclaimed Theodore the presidential nominee of the new Progressive Party.

But in Baltimore a week later, as Alice sat in her evening gown at the Democratic convention, she knew that only Woodrow Wilson's loss would give her father a real chance at the presidency. Everyone in the family, including her younger brothers and cousins, was working in Theodore's campaign, but she was powerless to help him, muted as she was by her decision that she could not fight for both her liberal father and her conservative husband. Archie and Nicholas, instructed to keep Theodore exercised, played tennis, hiked, and chopped wood with him in Oyster Bay while Alice's uselessness filled her with "bottled-up savagery." She said later that she had been plagued by stomachaches and reduced to a diet of Vichy water and scrambled eggs.

Probably Alice envied Champ Clark's seventeen-year-old daughter, Genevieve, who was free to stamp her foot in fury. As soon as William Jennings Bryan claimed that Champ Clark had sold out to Tammany Hall, Genevieve demanded that her father's managers make him come to the convention and defend himself. The delegates were enchanted by Genevieve, who was quite pretty, and carried her around the armory on their shoulders.

Unlike Alice, Eleanor claimed not to be interested in the drama taking place on the convention floor. Well schooled in politics, she knew that Wilson's nomination could help Franklin's future and she understood the issues possibly at stake in the 1912 campaign. "If we are not going to find remedies in Progressivism," she said, "then I feel sure the next step will be Socialism." Nevertheless, in the middle of the convention, Eleanor left Baltimore with her three children for Campobello. She wrote later that she had been put off by the crowds and "appalled" when Champ Clark's daughter was carried around the hall. But there may have been another reason as well. Theodore was, as Kermit had put it, praying for Clark's nomination, while Franklin was campaigning for Woodrow Wilson. It troubled Eleanor to take sides against Theodore, Alice, and Kermit. Until now, the fact that Franklin was a Democrat and her uncle was a Republican hadn't mattered, because they embraced the same ideals. But Franklin's active support for Wilson had disturbed the nicely balanced equation, for a Democratic victory would mean Theodore's defeat. Eleanor wrote a friend that she wished "Franklin could be fighting now for Uncle Ted."

By Saturday, June 29, the Democratic convention was in serious disarray. Rumors swept the armory that the convention leaders were trying to find a dark horse to pass both Clark and Wilson. After four long days and nights, the heat had put the delegates and spectators into an "ugly mood," and they agitated the sweaty air with palm-leaf fans. It was so hot that white doves, released to encourage feelings of amity and concord, refused to fly.

Finally that evening, at a little after ten o'clock, a single Maryland delegate broke away from Champ Clark and went over to Woodrow Wilson. The hall erupted. Several hundred spectators wearing Clark buttons swarmed onto the convention floor. To the dismay of the Clark supporters, a hundred were yelling, "WE WANT WILSON!" Franklin had planted them. He had given Clark pins to Wilson loyalists when he learned that an armory gatekeeper had been bribed to let everyone who wore a Clark button enter the hall. Brisk hand-to-hand combat ensued between the Clark forces, real and fake, and the convention adjourned for the rest of the weekend.

The lone breakaway Maryland delegate may have been the small trigger of great change. On Sunday, 100,000 yellow telegrams supporting Wilson arrived at the armory. By Wednesday, July 3, it became apparent that in the battle for the presidency, the Republican incumbent, William Taft, would be facing two reform candidates: Democrat Woodrow Wilson and Progressive Party candidate Theodore Roosevelt.

FOR MONTHS, Alice had spent hours at a time languidly rocking on the porch of Sagamore Hill—like a boarder in a summer hotel, Edith thought. In her opinion, her stepdaughter's speech patterns, normally tart and crisp, had softened under the pre-election strain to the consistency of molasses. But one afternoon in July, Alice rocked furiously in her old wicker chair. Beside her, Theodore rocked as furiously. Except for Nick, who sat with them, the family kept a prudent distance. The three were holding a "court of justice" to decide whether she should attend the first convention of the new Progressive Party. Later, Alice remembered how sweet Nick and her father had been, but at the time she wept. They decided she could not go with Theodore, either to the convention or on the campaign trail, and she had promised to abide by their decision. It would not be fair to Nick, her father said. Her attendance would suggest that she was his Progressive daughter and not Nick's conservative Republican wife. Alice said it was a "frightful disappointment." Had she been allowed to travel with him, Alice would have been company for her father. A reporter on the campaign train was once struck by the sight of Theodore standing alone on the back platform at dawn. He had come out to wave at the people who had clustered on the shadowed prairie hoping to catch a glimpse of him. The picture drawn by the newsman would not have seemed lonely if Alice had been at Theodore's side, nearly as fixed in the American consciousness as he.

The newly created Progressive Party held its convention in Chicago the first week of August. The purpose was to nominate its candidate for-

*Theodore campaigning as the Progressive Party's
presidential candidate in 1912*

*Theodore's bloodstained shirt
after he was shot in Milwaukee
on October 14, 1912*

mally. Alice was conspicuously absent, and so were Franklin and Eleanor. Some family members claimed that Franklin only looked out for himself; that he refused, as other relatives had not, to sacrifice his political prospects to help Theodore. Their comments may have been engendered by competition among the cousins. Franklin was already highly visible in New York state politics, while his Republican cousin Teddy Robinson was just beginning to campaign for an assembly seat in the same state. And Theodore's eldest son was likely to choose a political career over life in the military, though even young Nicholas sensed Ted had not "inherited his father's flair for politics."

Theodore understood Franklin's political ambitions and respected his decision to build a future in the Democratic Party. Alice recalled that her father "liked Franklin very much and he was very helpful to him." Sometimes that meant counseling the young Democrat to keep his distance. "I am very anxious to see you and Franklin, whenever the chance offers," Theodore now wrote Eleanor, "but I do not want to compromise Franklin by being with him just at this time."

The day before the Progressive convention opened in Chicago, a reporter from the Republican newspaper the *New York Herald* remarked that someone could roll a hogshead through the lobby of the Congress Hotel and not hit a soul. The next day the same paper reported that convention managers were slashing the price of seats from twenty dollars to three to try to fill the hall. The comments were evidently prompted by political spite, for trains were busy bringing people to Chicago from nearly every state. Many wore red bandannas—the symbol of the Progressive Party—tied to the bands of their hats or knotted around their necks. The society magazine *Town and Country* found the Progressives a clean-cut, good-looking crowd. The girls in their "shirt-waists" were more appealing than the "millionairesses" at the Republican convention six weeks before— and there were more of them. Half the spectators at the Progressive convention were women, and some were even delegates. Many carried yellow VOTES FOR WOMEN banners. "Anything that the women of this country want," Theodore said with innocent vigor, "I want to give them." He supported women's suffrage, in the belief that the "average American is a pretty good fellow and that his wife is a still better fellow."

One day the *New York Herald* referred to the convention as a two-ring circus, and on the next, called it Theodore's one-ring show. Barbershop quartets sang, bands played, and barkers hawked their wares, but a seriousness of purpose lay beneath all the razzle-dazzle. The thousands who came—the intellectuals, farmers, shopkeepers, and schoolteachers—knew that the progressive movement was written in the blood of "plain people," of those who had managed to survive and those who had not. Theodore built his campaign on the dignity of the poorest person. "None of us," he said, "can really prosper permanently if there are masses among us who are debased and degraded." His championship of individual rights would contribute to a changed dynamic in American life. With minimum wages, social security, and workmen's compensation, it would be possible for people to become economically independent of their families. "You may not like Roosevelt, but it would be foolish to shut your eyes to the strength of the movement behind him," *Town and Country* cautioned its readers.

The anti-Roosevelt press fulminated against the "criminal egotism" that had led Theodore to form his own political party and try to win the presidency for what amounted to a third term. They claimed that his was not a new political party at all, but a conspiracy to seize the government and establish a lifelong dictatorship. Once Theodore had reinstalled himself, they warned, he intended to "take the butter off the bread of the wealthy and spread it upon the crusts of the poor." A rumor went around that he wanted to require railroad companies—the richest of the monopolies—to furnish free food to the residents of those counties through which their trains traveled.

In his address to the Progressive convention on August 6, 1912, Theodore's wishes were less radical. He characterized the old political parties as "husks" with no "soul" and called for wages high enough "to make morality possible." Yet Theodore could not resist raising his endeavor to biblical heights. "We stand at Armageddon," he declared, "and we battle for the Lord."

MORE THAN ONE PERSON in New York City glanced up at the tower of the Metropolitan Life building—then the world's tallest— during the summer of 1912 and wondered in what direction its searchlight would point after the votes were counted in November. In those slower days, this was the way to learn who had been elected president. If the horizontal beam lit the western sky, it meant that Theodore Roosevelt had won; if it pointed north, Woodrow Wilson was the victor; if to the east, William Taft had been reelected.

While the presidential candidates laced their way back and forth across the United States on their special campaign trains, Franklin climbed back into the old red Maxwell and bumped his way along the dirt roads of his district in pursuit of renomination for the state senate. "The hunt is on, and the beasts of prey have begun to fall," the young progressive Democrat said, echoing Theodore, who was hammering away at the struggle between the "plain people" and the "powers that prey."

On the evening of October 14, at the height of the campaign, Edith was sitting in a New York theater when Nicholas Roosevelt's brother Oliver slipped into a seat beside her. Patting the boy's knee fondly, she was shocked to find his body shaking uncontrollably. Her husband had just been shot in Milwaukee, Oliver told her, but Theodore's steel spectacle case, in his right breast pocket along with the speech he was about to make, had blunted the force of the bullet and saved his life. Theodore had gone ahead and delivered his speech. Dropping fifty bullet-riddled pages on the floor one by one as he finished reading them, he spoke to the crowd, the bullet lodged in his chest, for an hour and a half. Only then was he taken by train to Chicago, where Alice came out of her seclusion to visit him. Years later, she said she would never forget "those little green rooms in Mercy Hospital."

Within three weeks, Theodore was campaigning again, but Franklin had been forced to stop altogether. After winning unanimous renomination to the state senate, in mid-September he was confined at home with typhoid fever. He told Eleanor to get in touch with his newspaper friend Louis Howe, who planned a phantom campaign. He pledged Franklin's commitment to specific agricultural issues and sent farmers letters that appeared to have been personally typed. It marked the beginning of a life-long collaboration.

Not until Sara took Eleanor's temperature did anyone realize that she, too, had typhoid. Both young Roosevelts were now in bed. "She sees no one but Franklin," Sara told one of Eleanor's aunts, "not even me!" Their recovery took several months, and though Eleanor and Franklin missed the excitement of the 1912 campaigns, they probably enjoyed their time together. "I simply hated to have you go on Saturday," Eleanor had written Franklin when he left for a trip earlier that year. "I feel very much alone and lost," Franklin replied. "I can't tell you how I long to see you again."

Alice, in political quarantine, also missed out on the excitement of the campaign trail, but there was no compensating peace to be found at home. She spent hours on the phone that fall, keeping in touch with Progressive headquarters and having long, miserable conversations with her husband. Melancholy and resentful, she had joked to friends about "fomenting such trouble" with Nick so that she could leave him and join her father. Privately, she was serious. Nick was coming to be known as the greatest womanizer on Capitol Hill. But when Alice suggested divorce to her family, though they "didn't quite lock me up," she wrote later, they did tell her it was "not done. Emphatically."

Nick had his own problems. He was running for reelection to Congress in the first district of Ohio on a strong Republican ticket headed by his fellow Ohioan William Howard Taft. His mother and sisters were busily raising money for the president and were bitterly resentful of Theodore. "Everyone says that if the Hon. Nick Longworth had it all to do over again," one gossip sheet reported, "he would rather decamp for Siberia than become related to the human dynamo, Roosevelt." Nick's way out of his dilemma was to support neither Taft nor his father-in-law. The vigorous Roosevelt family found Nick's inaction intolerable. Edith wished Nick would "work for Taft, or do something! It is hard on everyone." Theodore wrote from Oyster Bay that "poor Alice is here. It is all horrid for her; she would feel better if Nick were strong for Taft."

On November 4, the beam on the tower of the Metropolitan Life building swung north to signal Democrat Woodrow Wilson's victory. For months, Alice had feared that her father would lose. She was relieved that his ordeal had come to an end, and disappointed that Nick had lost his congressional seat. Eleanor, who, out of loyalty to Franklin, had withdrawn from the uncle she had loved all her life, was saddened nonetheless by Theodore's defeat. Because Eleanor and Franklin were still too ill to go out, Sara went to Progressive Party headquarters in New York City on election night as a gesture of family unity.

Franklin won his reelection to the state senate, and Teddy Robinson was elected to the state assembly. Eleanor and Helen looked forward to spending time together in Albany. But within a few months the new Democratic president appointed Franklin his assistant secretary of the Navy, the same office Theodore had held fifteen years before. "It is interesting that you are in another place which I myself once held," Theodore told him. Franklin's new boss, Josephus Daniels, noted that "his distinguished cousin TR went from that place to the Presidency. May history repeat itself."

Eleanor teased Franklin about his swift political rise. She claimed that her mind reeled at the thought of what he might do next—"run for Governor, U.S. Senator, go to California! I wonder what you really will do!"

Wartime Washington

ONE DAY IN THE FALL OF 1913, Eleanor sat on the deck of a battleship and felt the roll of the sea beneath her. She had gone with Franklin, the Navy's new assistant secretary, to watch target practice, and out of pride she hid her seasickness. A young officer mistook her silence for boredom and asked if she would like to go up the new "skeleton mast"— the bony spine, spiraled by steel ladders, that climbed the sky for a hundred feet. By the time Eleanor had changed to dungarees and reached the top, her nausea was eased by the fresh salt wind.

For Franklin, sitting on a Navy ship with the wind whipping across Chesapeake Bay, the naval flags flying, and the officers standing at attention represented a childhood dream come true. He had wanted to become a naval officer ever since he had heard the sailing stories told him by his grandfather Warren Delano. James Roosevelt had discouraged the idea, claiming that an only son shouldn't spend long months at sea. Franklin had contented himself with building up a naval-history library and amassing an extensive collection of naval prints. At first, the Navy captains had been startled when Franklin asked to steer their ships. One said he thought no yacht club sailor would know how to take a destroyer through narrow channels; however well positioned, the ship pivoted at a point one third aft, and the stern's arc was twice that of the bow. When Franklin kept looking back as he steered to check the swing of the stern, the captain realized he was more than a white-flanneled sailor.

Franklin enjoyed the ships on Chesapeake Bay and his square, high-ceilinged office in the Navy Department, but he felt his future was best tied to his political record in New York. In the autumn of 1914, he took a brief leave of absence and sought his state's Democratic nomination for U.S. senator. He failed in the attempt, and after brushing off his loss with customary lightness, he settled down to business at the Navy Department. Franklin's mother, aware of the rivalries among the Roosevelt cousins, was relieved to have her son out of New York politics. She told Franklin that she knew things about Teddy Robinson from " 'away back' which I can't repeat but *he* is not a friend to you & I am glad you need never look to him for help in *anything*."

That summer the nation was caught up in disquieting news from abroad. The Balkan states were involving the European nations in their struggle to dominate one another. Austria-Hungary and Russia were separately cultivating different Balkan allegiances, while England and France had formed a diplomatic alliance against the growing strength of the German Empire. In late July 1914, Franklin was called back to Washington from Campobello, where he had been vacationing with Eleanor and their children. On July 28, Austria-Hungary declared war on Serbia, and Russia announced a general mobilization to protect Serbia. Germany declared war against Russia on August 1, France entered on Russia's side on August 3, and Great Britain followed the next day. The world had erupted and it was only a matter of time before the boundary lines of Europe would be drawn in the blood of millions of dying men.

At the Navy Department, Franklin was astonished to find that "nobody seemed the least bit excited about the European crisis." The day after Britain joined the conflict, President Woodrow Wilson declared America's complete neutrality. Franklin's boss, Josephus Daniels, although appointed to the post of secretary of the Navy, was deeply pacifist. "He totally fails to grasp the fact that this war between the other powers is going inevitably to give rise to a hundred different complications in which we shall have a direct interest," Franklin wrote Eleanor.

In his view, the Navy should draw its fleet together and operate it at the "highest state of efficiency." The Department didn't command a large budget, and Franklin concentrated on finding ways to economize. He traveled to every naval yard in the country and tried to make them self-sustaining; like Daniels, he insisted upon competitive bidding among private suppliers. Franklin's goal, as Theodore's had been before him, was to build more ships. But progress was slow. "Some fine day the State Department will want the moral backing of a 'fleet in being,'" he complained to Eleanor, "and it *won't be there*." Franklin set out to educate the American public about the need for a larger and stronger Navy. Wilson and Daniels were hesitant to make warlike declarations, and Franklin risked a great deal in the fall of 1914 when he wrote a memo stating that the Navy needed an additional 18,000 men above the limit placed by Congress. Without them, thirteen battleships would remain out of commission.

The president continued to temporize, even after a German submarine torpedoed the British passenger ship *Lusitania* in May 1915. Theodore complained of a "thick streak of yellow in our national life," but Wilson managed to parlay his campaign slogan, "He kept us out of war," into reelection in 1916. Theodore thought Wilson was waiting until public opinion compelled the country to fight, but he believed a president should lead his people—if necessary, into combat. One evening in March 1917, nearly three years after the war began, Franklin, Theodore, and a few other influential politicians dined together at New York's Metropolitan Club. It was suggested that as a group they publicly praise the Wilson administration. Theodore disagreed, Franklin noted in his diary, saying they should instead make a "vigorous demand about future course." He added that he "backed T.R.'s theory."

Nick Longworth had been reelected to Congress in 1914, and he and Alice were back in the capital. Some of the cousins spent days and sometimes whole nights that spring listening to the intensifying debates in Congress over America's possible entry into the war. When Alice returned to her house on M *Street* after a month away, she immediately invited Franklin and Eleanor to lunch, and they caught her up on all of the news.

The Roosevelts relished their common endeavor. "We all felt we were part of a great crusade," Corinne Jr. said. With one important difference. Franklin's frustrations with Wilson stemmed from the president's unwillingness to declare war; the Oyster Bay relatives had detested Wilson ever since he had defeated Theodore in 1912. From Alice, typically: "Horrible man, we all said, chasing after women and then saying his prayers before leaping into bed with them."

On April 2, 1917, Eleanor and Franklin walked in the rain over to the Capitol Building to hear the president address Congress. The Germans had just sunk three American merchant ships, and Wilson's statement "The world must be made safe for democracy" was made to great applause. Four days later, the United States declared war on the German Empire.

Franklin tried to prod Secretary of War Josephus Daniels into swift military action, and politicked for action for himself as well. On an official trip to France, he told a French gathering that he would address them in an accent made famous by his cousin Theodore: "Roosevelt French—perfectly awful." He insisted on going to the front at Château Thierry, and when a young officer showed him a route that would ensure safe passage, Franklin's response was scathing. The point of the trip, he told the officer, was not his safety; months later, Franklin recommended against the young man's advancement.

Meanwhile, Theodore was "*very* proud" of Franklin for his wish to leave the Navy Department and go to the front. He wrote him that "Eleanor will tell you of our talk about your plans." Eleanor remembered that "Uncle Ted was *always* urging Franklin to resign," but that her husband's superiors, President Wilson and Secretary Daniels, refused to allow it. They said they needed him in Washington. Because the country was at war, the Secret Service suggested that Franklin carry a revolver on his walk to work, but after trying a shoulder holster for a few days, he took it off. In an overcoat, it took him thirty seconds to pull out his gun, aim, and fire— too long to defend himself, and not the form of combat he craved.

Theodore was as eager as his cousin to go to war. Twenty years before, he had charged up San Juan Hill in Cuba with troops he had raised from the plains of the Dakotas and the men's clubs in New York. Now he enlisted Alice's help in arranging an extensive agenda of political meetings. One night he dropped by Eleanor and Franklin's house and frisked with their children; then, waving his arms, he strode back and forth before their "blazing fire," young James remembered, and asked Franklin to put in a good word for him with Secretary of War Newton D. Baker.

A few days later, Theodore went off to the White House and asked Wilson to allow him to lead a division in Europe. Franklin and Eleanor waited at Alice's house, hoping for good news. But when her uncle returned, Eleanor saw that he was "in a very unhappy mood." Theodore sensed, rightly, that the decision would be no. Months later, when the German Army seemed about to take the Russian city of Petrograd, Franklin told Daniels with rare anger, "We ought to have sent TR over with 100,000 men. This would not have happened." Corinne Jr. later wrote that Theodore became a "great controversial figure" when he took a stand against Wilson and that "all our clan followed him with great enthusiasm." But Eleanor was afraid the Roosevelt family was "being torn" by the conflict between her uncle and the president. Like Franklin, she "hated to have him [Theodore] disappointed and yet I was loyal to President Wilson."

The fact that both Theodore and Franklin were demanding to fight led Josephus Daniels to question the younger man's motives in wanting to go to war. "Theodore Roosevelt had gone up that way," Daniels said. His heroism in Cuba had solidified his political career, and Daniels suspected that combat for Franklin was one more way to mimic his cousin's political ascent. "I always thought he had this in mind."

Kermit, on the way to the front with his brothers, wrote Franklin, "The hats of all are off to you for the way you've handled things in the navy." But Franklin envied his Roosevelt relatives. Even his young brother-in-law, Hall, had signed up, with Quentin, for the newly formed Air Force. A reporter admiringly described Franklin in his office—hard at work in his

A line of American soldiers in
Germany, led by Lieutenant Colonel
Ted Roosevelt, Theodore's son,
in World War I

Quentin Roosevelt and a fellow
soldier during World War I

Theodore and his family at Sagamore Hill in December
1917, the last Christmas they would all spend together

The Franklin Roosevelt family in about 1917

shirtsleeves, jumping up quickly to grab his cigarettes from his jacket pocket, his eyes "intensely blue" in the haze of smoke. But a neat desk in the Navy Department with its vase of fresh flowers could not approach the blood-race of battle.

ONCE THE UNITED STATES had entered the war, thousands of soldiers poured into Washington during the summer of 1918 as the country mobilized. Eleanor helped Addie Daniels, the Navy secretary's wife, to organize the Naval Red Cross. She worked twelve-hour days in the tin-roofed Red Cross canteens at railway sidings, so caught up in her work that she regretted not having time to spend with Franklin. One day she pressed him into service, packaging sandwiches and making coffee for the troop trains, and reported that he had enjoyed it.

Toward the end of the war, Eleanor began to visit injured sailors. Shocked by the conditions in the naval wards of St. Elizabeth's Hospital, and moved by the suffering she saw there, she appealed to her friend Franklin K. Lane in his capacity as secretary of the interior. Despite a number of bureaucratic obstacles, she was instrumental in increasing the hospital's budget. Eleanor's competence did not surprise Alice. She said her cousin did things "a little better than anyone else" during the war years. Nor did she find Eleanor's independence surprising. Alice told an interviewer years later that her cousin had "always wanted to be somebody in her own right, not just as Franklin's wife." Eleanor's initiative mirrored Franklin's attitude toward Josephus Daniels and Woodrow Wilson. Both young Roosevelts "started out with the idea that all older people were wrong," their cousin-by-marriage David Gray maintained. He believed one of the strongest bonds between Eleanor and Franklin was their shared distrust of the conservative attitudes of their parents' generation.

The war effort consumed the capital, and even Alice felt momentarily drawn to help Eleanor in the cooking shacks, though her cousin quickly noticed that she didn't like "scrubbing and ironing." But when the Army Secret Service man Colonel Marlborough Churchill suggested that Alice might spy for her country, she jumped at the chance. According to her, the mission involved planting listening devices in the house of a German-American woman whose uncle in Budapest was eager for war news. Sent to reconnoiter, Alice discovered a mattress swinging hammocklike in the bedroom. She suggested bugging it. As part of the intrigue, Franklin contrived to get misleading documents into the household in hopes that the German-American lady would send the false data to her interested uncle.

Franklin was not the putative spy's only source for inside information. Bernard Baruch, who knew everything worth knowing in the capital, came to call on her. Swinging with Baruch on her bugged bed, the lady asked him how many locomotives had been sent to Romania—"or something like that," Alice said. She claimed that she had listened to their conversation herself, and had heard the woman tell Baruch, as the hammock swung more amorously, "You are a coward, you don't dare look."

Alice welcomed the diversion of espionage. She lived with Nick in a handsome brick house, caught in a difficult marriage. Her diary shows that she had struggled for some time to understand what had drawn them together, and that she had concluded they were both pulled in two directions, good and bad. But Alice now believed Nick was trying to be good, while she still wanted to be bad. After they spent time at the family house in Ohio, Alice noted in her diary how close Nick was to his mother, how much he wanted to be a good son.

"I was never a 'nice young girl,'" Alice wrote, by contrast. "My instincts and desires were at least half in the other direction." She thought that her husband's wish to be good was beginning to win out, while she was hell-bent on becoming worse than ever. Though Alice recognized their incompatibility, she didn't know what to do about it. In one entry in her diary, she contemplated an affair with an unnamed "oriental-faced acquaintance." In another, she decided to remain loyal to Nick and help him shape a great career. And so it went. Eventually, Alice's name was linked romantically with that of Senator William E. Borah; when, on February 14, 1925, at the age of forty-one, she gave birth to a daughter, Paulina, the baby was widely thought to be his.

During the war years, the Nicholas Longworths and the Franklin Roosevelts entertained each other often in Washington. Alice was "looking fairly well" and was "very nice," Eleanor reported to her friend Isabella Selmes after a Longworth dinner party. But though Alice's house was charming and she was a born hostess with "an extraordinary mind," Eleanor thought "the bluebird" of happiness always had to be searched for "in some new and novel way."

Quite strikingly, Alice agreed with Eleanor's appraisal. "I always wanted to know about everything—personally," she wrote in her diary. "So I don't imagine I could ever be any too absolutely contented, but sometimes gloriously happy."

Alice turned up regularly at Eleanor and Franklin's dinner parties, but Nick rarely accompanied her. She said that he preferred things to be jolly, by which she meant that he drank heavily and flirted outrageously. He liked to be around "good-looking girls" and didn't find Eleanor attractive, Alice said. Nor did he care particularly for Franklin. Other guests remembered their evenings in the Roosevelt home with pleasure. The couple was well traveled, Eleanor was fluent in French, and because they often reached out to foreign visitors, they were known for keeping "an open house."

When Eleanor and Franklin first came to Washington, they rented their aunt Bye's house at 1733 N Street. It was referred to as the "Little White House," because Theodore had stayed there briefly when he had first assumed the presidency. Franklin liked the brick house partly for its association with Theodore and his political ascent, but Eleanor's friends were drawn to its "family atmosphere." They found their former classmate "so maternal" and "as dear, as affectionate, as simple and spontaneous" as she had been at seventeen.

In 1918, Eleanor and Franklin's children ranged in age from twelve to two years old: Anna, then four boys—James, Elliott, Franklin Jr., and

John. Later, Eleanor would write that they had a difficult childhood because she hadn't been a good mother. Much would be made, in the years to come, of the story that Eleanor, acting on the belief that fresh air was healthy for babies, had strung up a crib box outside a bedroom window. Several friends said that they had admired her forward-thinking approach to child care at the time, but a neighbor was shocked.

Eleanor's mistakes were compounded by the fact that Franklin often ceded his authority to his mother. Eleanor thought the two were so quick to quarrel that Franklin had decided to let his mother have her way in order to be left in peace. As the years went by, Eleanor noticed that Franklin became reluctant to visit Hyde Park, and she concluded that, although they loved each other, mother and son were "too much alike" to get along well.

But while Franklin allowed Sara to give his children too many toys and later, too many cars, during the war years he drew a line between him and his mother. It began as a discussion about the Hyde Park house and ended, hours later, in a bitter and far-ranging argument. Franklin spoke with feeling about the liberal economic and social issues that lay close to his heart—and that deeply offended Sara. There was no give in Franklin then, nor would there be, on politically significant matters.

In Washington, when the weather was fine, the family had their breakfast outside in Bye's little walled garden. Eleanor particularly enjoyed those spring mornings, seated across the table from her husband. When they were in New York or Hyde Park, her mother-in-law occupied the chair opposite Franklin. Sara's usurpation would end only when she demanded to be seated in the hostess's place at official White House dinners and the chief of protocol refused to allow it. But Bye's house in Washington was too small to accommodate Sara for more than a few days at a time. The young Roosevelts spread Hyde Park butter on their toast and stirred Hyde Park cream into their coffee, but Sara herself was safely at bay. When Eleanor and Franklin sat beneath Bye's rose arbor, they faced each other.

PART FOUR

SCHISMS

1918–1924

Lucy Mercer

LATE IN THE SUMMER OF 1918, two of the cousins' marriages appeared to be having difficulties. Alice might believe in Nick's improvement, but his public lapses mortified her. Bawdy humor about the Longworth marriage often rollicked across the capital, usually followed by one pursed-lipped disclosure or another—that Alice had plucked a pair of lace panties not her own from the dining room chandelier, or had opened a bathroom door and stumbled upon Nick groping one of her close friends. When a congressman remarked that Nick's shiny bald head looked just like his own wife's bottom, Nick, without an instant's pause, replied, "So it does."

Increasingly, Teddy Robinson was leading his wife, Helen, "a merry life" with much drinking, Eleanor and Franklin's daughter, Anna, recalled. Her father didn't like "getting crocked," and so he didn't approve of the Robinsons' wild parties. Nor did Eleanor, for Teddy's drinking habits reminded her of Hall's, and revived memories of her father's.

By contrast, Eleanor and Franklin's marriage seemed idyllic. Franklin's political future appeared full of promise, while Eleanor was so busy with her volunteer work and her children that she needed more help at home. In the winter of 1913, she and Franklin had hired a young society woman, Lucy Mercer, as her social secretary. It was said of Lucy that her

155

voice had the quality of "dark velvet" and that all men fell in love with her. Unbeknownst to Eleanor, Franklin was among them.

In the years to come, Alice liked to describe how the flirtation between Franklin and Lucy began, probably during the summer of 1916 when Eleanor was on Campobello with the children. Making full use of her gift for mimicry, Alice said a friend would telephone Franklin and say, in a fake European accent, "I haf some body here who vants to talk to you and that you vould like to see." The woman would then bring Lucy around for tea.

Alice bragged to an interviewer many years later that she had encouraged the romance. She had teased Franklin about driving in the country with "the lovely lady" and had invited them to dinner one summer night because, she said, "he deserved a good time, he was married to Eleanor." Alice had admired Eleanor since childhood, had wished at times to be as noble, but she always found herself wanting. Now, out of envy, she played with Eleanor's marriage like a toy. But even Alice's malice went only so far. She insisted that the relationship between Franklin and Lucy had been exaggerated. She told an interviewer that it had been a mere "lonely-boy-meets-girl thing . . . the snipped-off lock of hair. That kind of thing." Alice claimed "it wasn't much of an affair, as good old Washington went," and she wished it could be put in capital letters that "I DO NOT THINK THAT ANYTHING EVER HAPPENED."

But in July 1917, while Franklin was writing Eleanor that "I really can't stand that house all alone without you," he was also describing outings he took with Lucy. One rainy day, he invited her and a few other friends to join him aboard a naval yacht on the James River. They visited several houses on the riverbank, and everyone ran back and forth to the *Sylph* "drenched to the skin," Franklin wrote his wife. Eleanor began to be anxious. A hot summer day and a beautiful young woman in light, wet clothes laughing and running with her husband down to the river and onto a boat sailing in the rain—where had it led?

Not far, Franklin's distant Oyster Bay relative Joseph Alsop concluded years later. Having considered the romance at length, Alsop wrote that Franklin's code—the code of his particular day in his particular group—permitted flirtations, evening sails, and dinner parties, but that he would bed a woman who was his social equal seemed unlikely. "The ways of the group both Franklin Roosevelt and Lucy Mercer came from," Alsop maintained, bore no resemblance to those of England, where "lovers were discreetly given neighboring rooms in big country houses." Yes, for a year or two, Franklin and Lucy sailed together and drove together to visit friends. "But that," Alsop wrote, "was that, beyond any reasonable doubt." Gladys Saltonstall Brooks, a member of Franklin's circle of friends, agreed. Everything was "very proper" in those days, she said. "You had a so-called affair, but you held yourself in check."

The romance was "little talked about" publicly at the time—other than by Alice—because people had "too much respect for Eleanor." And no "paper trail," as one historian put it, has led to anything indicating that Lucy and Franklin's relationship was physically passionate. Or to anything indicating that in 1918, his love for Lucy was greater than his love for Eleanor. Franklin never made his feelings known. If he told anyone, it went unrecorded. It is interesting to note that it is not facts, but recognition of the universal desire in human nature to possess that which is loved, that substantiates the conclusion people draw, that Franklin's romance with Lucy was physical.

Eleanor did not discover his love affair with her social secretary until September 1918, when it had been going on for at least a year. The story goes that, unpacking Franklin's bags after his return from a trip abroad, she found love letters from Lucy tucked among his clothes. No one else claims to have seen the letters, nor can they be found today, but with Eleanor's discovery, she and Franklin and Lucy became unwitting characters in a family melodrama.

Lucy, the Other Woman, was from an old Southern family. Her smile was compared to that of the *Mona Lisa,* and Alice described her as having "a really lovely-shaped small head." Anna Roosevelt believed Lucy's real attraction was more subtle. "Giving a man her undivided attention," twenty-seven-year-old Lucy listened quietly and asked "good, sensitive questions," Anna said. But Lucy was also Roman Catholic, and her religion forbade her to marry a divorced man with five young children.

While Franklin, the Seducer, was probably not surprised to find himself attracted to soft-spoken Lucy, he had always encouraged Eleanor to argue with him and voice her own opinions. The independence he had fostered in his wife may have made him lonely enough to have an affair with Lucy; but it's doubtful that at thirty-six, Franklin would want to break the tie he and Eleanor had shared since childhood, if only because his steady Dutch heritage was a matter of pride to him. In his social circle, as well, there was considerable prejudice against Catholicism.

Eleanor, the Betrayed, was guided in her marriage by the examples set by the strong women she had known as a child. Edith's hand in Theodore's had been firm as well as loving, and Eleanor's other Oyster Bay aunts were yeasty and self-sufficient. Thirty-four-year-old Eleanor hadn't been overwhelmed by Franklin in the more than dozen years they had been married, and a close friend was struck by how very deeply she understood him.

Years after the crisis in the Roosevelt marriage, members of the family gave their own versions of how the drama among the three characters had finally been resolved. Alice claimed that Franklin didn't want a divorce and Eleanor didn't want to make a fuss about the romance. She said it was Sara—like Queen Victoria, "shocked but delighted"—who "made too much of it." Sara came to Eleanor and "wanted to know what was she going to do about Franklin and Lucy Mercer."

Corinne Jr.'s version was that Franklin asked Eleanor for a divorce and that she was "quite prepared" to grant him one. But according to Corinne Jr., Sara then threatened that "if he got a divorce, he would not get a penny from her," and so he persuaded Eleanor to remain in the marriage.

Franklin and Eleanor's daughter, Anna, had yet another version, claiming that Sara never threatened her son at all. Her mother told her that Franklin hadn't wanted a divorce, "because it would destroy his career." But Anna didn't believe it. She thought her mother, convinced of her inad-

Lucy Mercer, after her marriage to Winthrop Rutherfurd

In the aftermath of his romance with Lucy Mercer, Franklin, assistant secretary of the Navy, and Eleanor review the U.S. fleet on its return from Europe in December 1918.

Eleanor holds Franklin's arm on the beach at Campobello in about 1920.

equacy as a wife, had used the story to "punish herself." Anna also took issue with the rumor among Lucy's friends that Eleanor had refused to "step aside" and give Franklin a divorce. She said her father might have implied something along those lines "as a way of putting off Lucy." Decades after the affair, Anna told a biographer that a few Oyster Bay relatives had been envious of Eleanor and her good-looking husband, particularly when he went into politics. Jealousy, she warned, could have rendered their various interpretations of the romance suspect.

It remains to integrate the Roosevelts' different, colorful melodramas into an account of what probably took place when Eleanor confronted Franklin with Lucy's letters. Most likely, as Alice thought, Sara got wind of Franklin's romance and asked Eleanor what she proposed to do about it. As a result of that conversation, Sara told Eleanor's sister-in-law with considerable surprise that she realized "Franklin did not want the divorce"; that, rather, it was Eleanor who "would not stay where she wasn't wanted." After "much conferring," the cousins' aunt Corinne said, Eleanor and Franklin decided to remain married. Probably he promised not to see Lucy again, although, as with all of these stories, there is no proof of that.

What is documented is that Eleanor thought it was better for a couple to separate than to "lead a quarrelsome life," and a few relatives and friends have agreed that Franklin didn't want to hurt his wife "any more than he already had." As Anna would put it in the language of a later generation, her father did not want to "bust this thing up," and her mother "loved the guy deeply."

What Sara intended to accomplish with her apparently needless threats was to place herself center stage, thereby suggesting that Eleanor could not save her marriage alone. According to Alice, Sara remained loyal to Eleanor but did not lament her daughter-in-law's difficulties. She was "angrily loyal, but pleased. Not averse to a little bit of one-upmanship," Alice said. One of Eleanor's friends concurred: "That old lady . . . hides a primitive jealousy of her daughter-in-law which is startling in its crudity."

In the aftermath of the affair, Anna sometimes found her mother slumped in a chair in her bedroom. Eleanor described herself as too sensitive, for she withdrew when she was hurt. But slowly she realized that to draw away from Franklin would end their marriage. Eleanor might have been speaking to herself when she once scolded an overly sensitive friend: "You simply cannot be so easily hurt, life is too short to cope with it!"

Alice thought that for a while Eleanor was resentful of Franklin's love affair, but Corinne Jr. marveled at her calm. "I have never seen Eleanor disturbed in my life," she said. Nonetheless, there were times when it was not possible to maintain the united front so important to both Eleanor and Franklin. A few photographs from the period show her to be sad and remote, and he lacks his usual ebullience. But such moments were rare. A friend, chancing upon the couple in Europe a few months after the romance ended, found them "on top of the wave—young and full of vigor." Eleanor appeared confident and outgoing, making new friends and visiting her old Allenswood schoolmates in London. When she came down with pleurisy, she claimed to be in a "rage" when Franklin, after taking her temperature, forbade her going out to dinner.

"She wasn't disturbed; he wasn't disturbed" was Corinne Jr.'s succinct description of the emotional balance that gave the couple room to heal. After their ordeal, Eleanor and Franklin resembled nothing so much as a pair of Thoroughbreds moving forward in matched, unbroken stride, each anticipating and following the other. They developed, one of their sons said, an intuition about each other.

In 1919 Lucy Mercer became engaged to Winthrop Rutherfurd. She worried that Franklin might learn of her coming marriage too indirectly, and so she enjoined a friend to tell him. Mrs. Frank Polk arranged to have tea with the Roosevelts, but found no opportunity to speak to Franklin alone. She was obliged, finally, to blurt out the news to Eleanor in a voice that carried. As Joseph Alsop tells the story, "Roosevelt started like a horse in fear of a hornet." This second-long reaction remains one of few indicators of Franklin's feelings for Lucy at the time of their love affair. Otherwise, he was opaque.

Later Eleanor mused about how easy it was to "drift apart and drift together with someone else." She had been too busy with her children and her volunteer work to spend much time with Franklin; Lucy, as Eleanor's social secretary, had been considered almost a member of the family. Looking back, Eleanor commented on what she believed to be a basic difference between the sexes. "The act of being physically unfaithful seems much less important to the average man," she wrote, and he finds it "hard to understand why the woman he loves looks upon it as all important."

But explanations, no matter how reasonable, don't heal a broken heart. As she had done before in her life, Eleanor looked within herself to gain the strength to go on. She took walks in Rock Creek Park, where she often paused beside the bronze figure by Augustus Saint-Gaudens that Henry Adams had commissioned in memory of his dead wife. Like Eleanor, Clover Adams had known the pain of a husband's betrayal, and Washingtonians called the statue *Grief*. When the story of Franklin's love affair became known, people assumed that shared sadness had drawn Eleanor to the bronze figure, but that wasn't so. In the years to come, Eleanor often showed the statue to friends. The woman's hand was strong, she pointed out. Her attitude conveyed complete repose. The cloaked figure, a hood framing her face, gave the impression not of grief, she said, but of a woman who had achieved "absolute self-mastery." Eleanor as a child had grasped the reins of her pony and decided to master her fears. As an adult, she mastered herself.

Eleanor continued to have faith in the transcendence of romantic love despite the pain she had suffered at its hand. When years later she read *For Whom the Bell Tolls*, Ernest Hemingway's tale of passionate lovers, she wanted to praise it in her newspaper column. Her assistant was appalled. She found it inappropriate for the president's wife to agree with Hemingway that three days of "full and perfect living" outside the accepted social mores was worth more than a lifetime of "halfliving" within them.

But Eleanor knew her own mind. "Only those who love," she maintained, "really live."

Peace Treaties

FRANKLIN AND ELEANOR spent Christmas of 1918 in Washington, but the holiday was still safely wrapped in the traditions of Hyde Park and Tivoli—in the rituals of their childhood. Well-worn custom eased the pain caused by Franklin's affair, though other Christmases had been more intimate. That December, Eleanor, pitying the wounded men in the military hospitals, invited twelve soldiers and twelve sailors to join them for the tree lighting, supper, and Christmas carols. The atmosphere within the household may have been subdued, but it wasn't rancorous. Eleanor was beginning to find shadings and complexities in love where before she had seen only black and white. "No one loves two people in exactly the same way," she would say years later, "but one may love two people equally and yet differently."

On Long Island on Christmas Day, an air of sadness hung over the few family members gathered in Oyster Bay. "They have all gone away from the house on the hill," Edith wrote. Ted and Kermit were still overseas, and her youngest son, Quentin, had been killed in combat, flying one of the new airplanes over German lines in France; Theodore said his wife would carry the wound "green to her grave." The First World War had ended in November, but of the brothers, only Archie, who had been invalided out of

Franklin, nominee in 1920 for vice president, with Eleanor and their children, from left, Anna, James, John, Elliott, and Franklin Jr.

Theodore in 1918, shortly before his death, holding his granddaughter Edith Derby

Theodore's son Archie in his World War I uniform

the Army in Europe, was able to join the family. Their grief over Quentin's death was mixed with concern about Theodore. Abscesses and fevers, recurrences of infections he had contracted on his wilderness journeys abroad, had plagued him for years. After having been hospitalized for more than a month, Theodore had been allowed, finally, to come home on Christmas Day.

On December 25, icicles hung from the veranda roof, and the house let in the winter wind as it always had; but fires blazed in the hearths, and the table was set for the holiday meal. Alice had spent her childhood in that dining room with political life, incarnate in her father, glowing and bumping around her. Then, his excitement had been for her like the wide December sky over Sagamore—all she knew, so scarcely noticed. But now, Alice was riveted. The policies of President Woodrow Wilson—the man who had bested her father in the 1912 campaign and who had won again in 1916—were being discussed at the family Christmas table.

It alarmed Theodore that the president wanted to tie the idea of an international body—a League of Nations—to the peace treaty for World War I. Wilson had sailed for Europe on December 3, 1918, for the Paris Peace Conference; in hand was his blueprint for appending a League of Nations to the terms of peace. For America to surrender its autonomy to another governing entity struck Theodore as both dangerous and unconstitutional. The country appeared to be with him. Nearly ten million men had died as a result of the war, among them more than one hundred and fifteen thousand U.S. troops dispatched in the last year. Many considered Europe no longer America's concern. Theodore spent Christmas Day writing letters, exhorting his followers in Congress to quash the possibility of a super body. Despite his illness, he worked at his usual frenetic pace, undaunted by the warning that if he did not slow down, he might spend the rest of his life in a wheelchair. He could work that way, too, he said.

But only days later, on January 6, 1919, Theodore died in his sleep of an embolism at the age of sixty. "The old lion is dead," Archie cabled his brothers overseas. He was buried in the winter light of Oyster Bay, without eulogy, music, or military honor. It was a stark leave-taking, of a piece with

Theodore's deliberate fondness for plain-coated simplicity in affairs of state. He had worn his black frock coat to King Edward's funeral, and probably he wore it at his own, as his coffin covered with snow-flecked pine boughs moved in silence through the crowd of mourners. The news came as a "shock" to Franklin, on his way to Europe with Eleanor to join the Wilsons. He had heard that Theodore was better, he told Josephus Daniels, and "after all not old." Eleanor wrote sadly in her diary, "Another great figure off the stage."

"My eyes," Edith wrote months later, "begin to fail from tears."

League business had occupied Theodore until the last, and Alice seized the thought that she would honor her father's memory by battling Wilson and his plan. It seemed a tall order for a thirty-five-year-old woman in 1919, but Alice had spent years in Washington detecting political trends and keeping her father informed of every new development. The year before, Theodore had asked Alice to make sure Will Hays became the chairman of the Republican National Committee; after hours on the telephone she had been instrumental in carrying out her father's wish. Now Alice wielded her considerable influence in a highly personal fight against Wilson. She converted the Longworth house into a meeting place for her fellow League protesters. Some newspapers labeled the dissidents—among them Senators William E. Borah, Philander Chase Knox, and Frank Brandagee—the "Battalion of Death," because they were refusing to approve the treaty for a war in which a generation of men had been killed. Alice was named the "colonel of death," as the result of her attempt to consolidate Theodore's loyalists with other influential people in order to forestall the ratification of the peace treaty.

The issue was hotly debated in the Senate over many months, and Alice appeared in the visitors' gallery nearly every day. Finally, on March 19, 1920, the Senate sent both the peace treaty and the charter of the League of Nations back to the White House unapproved. "It was entirely personal politics designed purely to annoy," Alice said disingenuously of her victory, never wishing to put anything other than her worst foot forward. "We were against the League because we hated Wilson, who was a Family Horror. He couldn't do any good in our eyes because he had beaten Father."

ONE DAY SEVERAL MONTHS LATER, during the 1920 Democratic National Convention in San Francisco, Franklin, who was a New York delegate, suddenly grasped the back of the chair in front of him and vaulted effortlessly over four rows of seats in order to reach the speaker before the gavel came down on further debate. "It was the most wonderful athletic feat," Frances Perkins remembered. "Very graceful" and, she claimed, "unstudied." The next second Franklin had jumped onto the convention platform, demanding to be heard.

Franklin's leap achieved more than the speaker's platform. Perkins said that his "insistence" impressed people and created "an immediate following . . . for him. He was somebody." So much a somebody that, after the Ohio newspaperman James Middleton Cox had been nominated the Democratic presidential candidate, a delegate came running to the back of the hall where Franklin sat with friends. "They're nominating you! They're nominating you!" said the delegate excitedly. Franklin, still the Navy Department's assistant secretary, only replied, "You're kidding me," and walked back to his hotel. Later he professed astonishment on learning that he had been selected Cox's running mate—the Democratic candidate for vice president.

A different man would have found the coming campaign a gray prospect. The Republicans controlled both houses of Congress, and a stroke had crippled President Woodrow Wilson. Worse, when the candidates paid the stricken president a courtesy call, Wilson raised his head and said that the battle for the League of Nations could still be won. It seemed a dead issue in 1920, hardly the stuff to enliven a campaign, but Cox determined that as a gesture of solidarity with Wilson, he and Franklin would fight for the League.

The axe swing of political allegiance threatened to divide the Roosevelt family. Cox's decision pitted Franklin against his cousin Alice, because their campaign strategy was based on the policies of Theodore's longtime enemy. The battle was further fueled by Alice's resentment of Franklin for having followed Theodore so closely, from the New York legislature to the Navy Department, that she feared there would be no room for her brother Ted. Now Franklin had become a candidate for vice president, an office her father had also held, and Alice vowed to fight her cousin at every turn.

Had Theodore been alive, no doubt he would have reined in his fractious daughter. He would have found Alice's hostility disturbing, despite the fact that in part the reason for it lay with him. Theodore had encouraged the cousins to follow the example of his life as surely as he had exhorted them to follow him on hikes. Had they felt free to choose their own course, a few might have led different lives—Ted to head a line of soldiers, and Alice to find causes other than avenging her father's past and her brother's future.

From a campaign standpoint, Cox's idea of making the League of Nations an election issue was a bad one. Some people even thought it was madness, but Franklin was merely energized. He began a summer of intensive campaigning in which he made two trips out West and a third through the Northeast. Leaving from Chicago on August 10, he toured twenty states in two and a half weeks. In a single lap across Washington State alone, he spoke twenty-six times in two days, as exuberant a campaigner as Theodore ever was. Over and over, Franklin alerted people to the need for internationalism, saying that it was no longer possible to be "a hermit nation, dreaming of the past," no longer possible "to be in this world and not of it."

Eleanor, back East on Campobello, felt left out of the excitement. "Dearest dear Honey," she wrote, "I am positively hungry for news of you." Franklin was glad she planned to join him on his last campaign swing through the West. "I can't wait," he wrote her. "I miss you so much. It is very strange not to have you with me in all these doings." During the early

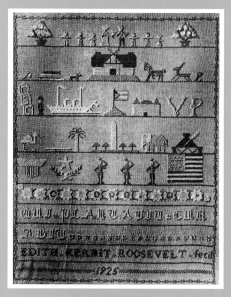

A sampler, sewn by Edith, commemorating
events in Theodore's life. From top:
children, Oyster Bay, political career,
hunting expeditions, Quentin's death, and
the other sons who served in World War I

Eleanor and Franklin, far right,
at the formal announcement of his Democratic
nomination for vice president in 1920

Democratic presidential candidate James M. Cox and Franklin,
vice-presidential hopeful, during the 1920 campaign

years of their marriage, Eleanor and Franklin had been together most of the time. He had confessed to her aunt Maude his selfishness in keeping Eleanor "too much with me," and making life "a trifle dull for her really brilliant mind and spirit." But more recently, with a houseful of children, Sara's disruptive presence, Eleanor's volunteer work, and the strains imposed by Franklin's affair, companionship had been rare. Political analysts are quick to explain that 1920 was the first year in which women could vote in a presidential election, and that was why Franklin wanted his wife at his side. But it was not why he later wrote his mother that "it has been a great comfort to have Eleanor." Like the old times in Albany, they were embracing the excitement of politics together.

Surefooted, Franklin used the Cox campaign to move beyond New York and beyond the Navy. Someone observed that he "played better on the big stage" than in small groups, gossiping and politicking with friends. It took a large arena—the breadth of America itself—to release in Franklin the eloquence that would one day sustain the nation through a depression and a world war. Once he had paused and searched for words; now they came to him easily. Franklin was nearly unstoppable. When he was to speak for ten minutes, he went on for twenty; half an hour could lengthen into an hour with all that Franklin had to say. Eleanor learned to sit near him and pull on his coat when he talked too long.

THEODORE'S SON TED had returned from the First World War a hero. Any man who loved the military, he said, wanted to take his place in the line whenever he saw troops on the march. Soldiering was what he loved, but politics was what he had been raised for. As a child, Ted had often suffered from headaches, and a doctor had finally told Theodore that unless he stopped pushing him, his son was in danger of having a nervous breakdown. A conscience-stricken Theodore had laid a lighter hand on Ted after that, but his touch remained. Ted's life was governed by a cruel combination of filial loyalty and the unspoken demands of others. His own wishes didn't seem to be a factor, and the strain was evident. A newsman remarked that the thirty-one-year-old's face looked as if it had outworn several bodies.

In 1919, Ted was elected to the New York State Assembly. He hoped to be named the candidate for governor at the state Republican convention that June in 1920, but failed to secure the nomination. At nearly the same moment, Franklin was selected as the Democratic candidate for vice president. Bye's son Sheffield Cowles Jr. said later that Ted always thought Franklin was "getting everything he [Ted] was entitled to." His situation was exacerbated by the fact that Theodore's fame had begun to redound to Franklin and not to him. FRANKLIN ROOSEVELT'S CAREER PARALLELS COUSIN TEDDY'S, headlines blared. COUSIN OF TR IS PICKED FOR SECOND PLACE.

Ironically, part of Franklin's popularity came from the public's ignorance and misconceptions. Eleanor, on the campaign train with Franklin, wrote her aunt Corinne apologetically, "I do see how annoying it must be to have people saying and thinking Franklin is a near relation of Uncle Ted's." Some people even believed that Franklin was Theodore himself: "We get asked if he's 'Teddy' frequently," Eleanor told Sara.

Ted felt that unless his cousin's connection with Theodore was severed, it would assure Franklin's political future and undermine his. The members of the Republican National Committee were also aware of Franklin's threat to Theodore's son, and concerned about the legacy of the Roosevelt name in the Republican Party. In an aggressive mood, they dispatched Ted out West in Franklin's wake to assert himself as his father's rightful heir. Newspapers quickly played up the battle between the two young Roosevelts. William H. Anderson, head of the Anti-Saloon League, publicly denounced the Republican plan to "show the people the real Roosevelt." He called it an "outrageous tragedy." When Franklin's presidential running mate, James Cox, sarcastically characterized Ted as a "misguided juvenile statesman," a reporter responded that the phrase should be applied to "quite a different Roosevelt, namely Franklin Delano Roosevelt."

Suspicion thickened in the Oyster Bay family that Franklin was, as

*Eleanor in about 1920, when Franklin
was making a run for the vice presidency*

Ted's gestures reminded many people of his father's.

*Nick and Alice, center, with, from left, President-elect Warren G.
Harding, John Weeks, and Mrs. Harding in Florida in 1921*

Louis Howe's son Hartley put it, "trading on the TR name, riding on TR's coattails." They were galvanized by the possibility that Franklin's ride might land him in national office. At a breakfast meeting during the Republican National Convention, the presidential candidate, Warren G. Harding, had pressed Alice for the "Roosevelt" party's endorsement. She bargained, saying she would support him if he would recommend Ted for the New York state governorship in 1924. The Oyster Bay Roosevelts despised Harding, but they campaigned for him in order to block Franklin's progress and ensure that Harding would help Ted. Eleanor asked her mother-in-law if she knew "that Alice is to go on the stump for Harding and that Auntie Corinne is to speak for him in Portland?"

On the campaign trail in September, wherever Franklin spoke for James Cox, Ted countered with a speech for Warren Harding. But suddenly, in Sheridan, Wyoming, Theodore's heir burst out against Franklin personally. "He is a maverick," Ted said. "He does not have the brand of our family." For some, his summary judgment was taken as a call for Franklin's expulsion from the Roosevelt clan. For others, like his cousin Nicholas, it served as a reminder that Oyster Bay Roosevelts shunned those relatives whom they considered disloyal.

Suddenly the Roosevelt name was no longer sufficient to define membership in the family. Hall's wife, Margaret, introduced to one distant Long Island cousin or another, would be asked if she was the "right" Roosevelt (from Oyster Bay) or the "wrong" one (from Hyde Park). Alice said later that her brother's words signaled "the beginning of very bad feeling" in the family. She wished that Franklin had just tossed off Ted's remark and said, "I wear no man's brand." But instead, he interpreted it "in the spirit it was meant (i.e. meanly) and got very annoyed."

Despite Franklin's anger, his response to Ted was indirect. A few days after his cousin's attack, on September 24, 1920, Franklin accused the Republicans of the greatest treachery. He alleged that the year before, Will Hays, whom Alice had helped install as the chairman of the Republican National Committee, had gathered a few key Republicans—among them League of Nations dissidents Borah, Brandagee, and Knox—in a secret conference. Franklin claimed that Will Hays had told the men to block the League and the treaty, not because either was inadequate, but because their approval would make heroes of Wilson and the Democratic Party and impossible to defeat in 1920. According to Franklin, Hays had told the men: Withhold approval of the League and the treaty, and the Democrats would lose the respect of the American people, and thus the election. "Partisan advantage was placed first," Franklin claimed; "restoration of peace to civilization was thrown into the discard." As long as the treaty remained unapproved, Franklin said, peace "hangs in the balance."

Not until many years later, in 1942, did Franklin reveal that the source of his inside information had been his cousin Alice Longworth. If what she said was true, Alice had been playing a role in a drama more extensive than the fight over the League of Nations. She was also trying to manipulate the outcome of a presidential election. It was a dizzying possibility, that the fates of both a world treaty and a national election were in part within her control. True or not, Alice got her wish. The Republicans won handily in November, and Warren G. Harding was elected president. Franklin had waged a fight reminiscent of Theodore's 1912 Progressive campaign: quixotic and intense, but doomed. Typically undaunted by defeat, Franklin told a friend that the campaign had been "a darned fine sail!"

Through both the presidential campaign of 1920 and the national debate over the League of Nations, politics had become a Roosevelt family affair. It seemed as if the old Oyster Bay dining room table now stood on a stage the size of America. Franklin, as Cox's running mate and a proponent of the League of Nations, sat on one side. Alice occupied the chair opposite as one of the League's strongest critics, and possibly with plans that had contributed to the Republican presidential victory. Ted, tense and ascetic, had drawn up to the table, too. Fighting against Franklin for his political life, he struggled to hear a father who no longer sat at the head of the table, no longer spoke.

Franklin's Polio

ALONG THE COAST of northern Maine, whitewashed houses scatter across green lawns uninterrupted by fences and stone walls. Cottages cling to the hillsides like barnacles and their small-paned windows edge on the sea. No McDonald's or neon signs or sun-shot expanses of plate glass disturb the green and white peace of Lubec, the town on the knoll that faces north toward Canada's Campobello Island.

Eleanor and Franklin's house on Campobello still looks as it did in August 1921. The ease of worn wicker and old flowered wallpaper comforts like a mother's lap, and a large megaphone is in the living room, waiting to summon children out sailing home to dinner.

On the second floor, a tour guide points to a narrow bedroom wide across the water. She says that Eleanor and Franklin occupied the room together until August 10, 1921. The double bed seems small—too small to accommodate the rumor that Eleanor and Franklin had stopped having sexual relations in 1916 to avoid another pregnancy. Perhaps Eleanor had stayed in the room next door, or Franklin? But the guide says no. Even after the last child, John, was born in 1916, and even after Franklin's affair with Lucy, she says, they continued to sleep in the room together.

If Eleanor and Franklin occupied the same bed, on whose authority do we have it that they were denied its pleasures? It was the Roosevelts' son Elliott who claimed that his parents stopped making love in 1916; he said his mother told him so years later. The Roosevelts' daughter, Anna, said that in 1926 her mother told her she had not been "sexually fulfilled" in her relations with Franklin, and that sex was a "cross to bear." The children's comments would do much to explain why Franklin had turned to Lucy Mercer in 1916, but it is impossible to assess the truth of their statements. Children are skittish and unreliable on the subject of their parents' sexual life. They are priggish and inclined to misconstrue. Even now it is unlikely that discussion between a parent and child about that parent's sex life would proceed frankly.

Such questions became moot, at least for a time, on the night of August 10, 1921. Franklin climbed the stairs to their bedroom without his dinner. He was chilled to the bone and feverish; Eleanor spent the night on the couch nearby and nursed him. After a long day of sailing, swimming, and running with the children, Franklin succumbed to a virus he had contracted, probably while visiting a Boy Scout encampment on the Hudson. In nearby New York City, 30 percent of the victims of the polio epidemic that summer were adults, and he was among them.

Nothing could be more poignant than the heart-stopping change in thirty-nine-year-old Franklin from fully vigorous to paralyzed. He lost the use of both his legs. Just the touch of a thin sheet on his body was agony, and he was in constant pain for months. As Joseph Alsop has observed, it is nearly unbearable to read the accounts of people who were close to Franklin in those days.

In dire moments, love remakes itself or runs away. Eleanor and Franklin's bedroom with its windows on the sea was anchored by his pain-racked, inert body. Now Eleanor's love was in her hands, turning him and changing his soiled linens. "Matter of fact" by nature, as she described herself—she took care of Franklin around the clock for weeks. Polio had immobilized his intestinal system, and it was Eleanor who placed the slender catheter in his penis and administered his enemas. Propriety would have the details of the scene go unmentioned, but history continues to question the quality of Eleanor and Franklin's love. Biographer Geoffrey Ward has conjectured that for Franklin, "this unavoidable business"—Eleanor's intimate touch—must have been "especially disagreeable" after his romance with Lucy Mercer. Yet Ward in the same biography writes in a footnote that "Eleanor evidently continued to perform these delicate tasks even after the arrival of Miss Edna Rockney, a trained nurse from New York." If not at Franklin's wish, then whose?

Eleanor once observed that her father with his problems had reminded her of Jesus in Michelangelo's *Pietà*. The image was more apt—and stunningly so—applied instead to Franklin and herself, for the famous statue shows Jesus lying in the arms of Mary, who cradles and protects the crucified Christ.

From the first moment of Franklin's illness, he and Eleanor displayed the kind of courage that was a distinct Roosevelt trait. Years later an interviewer marveled to Alice about Eleanor's self-discipline—modeled, he thought, on the way Theodore had transformed his childhood frailties into strength. "Franklin also had it," Alice said, with considerable understatement. For despite the pain in his body, people saw only his tossed head and his grin. Sara, arriving back from Europe, said in astonishment that "the atmosphere of the house is all happiness." Slowly, the children grew accustomed to their physically altered father. But one moment would startle them every year, at Christmastime. Franklin continued to place candles on the tree, but now his sons and daughter helped him, for he could only reach the lower branches.

As a boy, Franklin had inherited simple religious beliefs from the generations of Roosevelt men who had prayed in the little church in Hyde Park. He did not question his faith when polio struck, but he told one of his sons later that he thought God had abandoned him. It was a reasonable assumption for a vigorous man who would not leap four rows of chairs again. But because he did not doubt the existence of God so much as mourn His absence, Franklin kept to his faith, and the fact that it

Franklin sailing with his children and friends near Campobello Island in 1920

Franklin and Eleanor's house on Campobello Island

*The view from Franklin's
window at Hyde Park
and a few of his books*

remained intact after the worst of his ordeal was cause enough for him to continue. Franklin had believed in God through the worst, and now He was present to him again.

Years later, Harry Hopkins was one of Franklin's closest advisors in the White House, but he wanted to become even closer to him. Frances Perkins thought Hopkins wanted to be Franklin's closest friend. But some aspect of Franklin eluded Hopkins. He envied Franklin, and his envy made him sad; he knew he would never possess that nameless quality Franklin had. "There's something that that man's got," Hopkins burst out to Perkins one day.

"Why Harry," she said, "it's clear that he's got a relationship to God."

"Yeah, that's it," Harry said. "He falls back on something that gives him complete assurance that everything is going to be all right." For Franklin, God's absence had been only momentary; His presence gave life meaning. Unlike him, Eleanor was prey to periods of despair, a condition she shared with Theodore. According to Alice, her father's melancholy streak had not surfaced often, but it had been "noticeable when it did." She thought the tendency to depression ran in the Oyster Bay Roosevelt family—they all had it "to one degree or another." Her own was less, Alice thought, because she recognized it, but she had found Theodore's "very real. Very fatalistic." Like Theodore's, Eleanor's sense of urgency was her bridge across times of despair. Niece and uncle had concluded that only by working and by caring could they advance across the void. Owen Wister might have been describing Eleanor when he wrote of Theodore that he grasped "his optimism tight, lest it escape him in the many darknesses that rose around him all along his way."

Some of Franklin's biographers maintain that his bravery resulted from his fight against polio, but his children disagreed. Elliott wrote that of all the stories that proliferated about their father, the "most fanciful" was the one that gave polio the credit for having prodded Franklin into courage and ambition. It struck Elliott as ludicrous that some people had considered his father a "restless, flighty young man" before he fell ill and that in some "mysterious fashion, polio completely changed his nature." His brother James concurred, writing, "It was not polio that forged Father's character, but that it was Father's character that enabled him to rise above the affliction."

One day Nicholas Roosevelt watched Elliott settle Franklin too quickly in a car, then turn away. Elliott did not see his father topple over—nor hear him laugh. Nicholas thought "a thousand" others in Franklin's predicament would have lashed out in helpless anger, at himself or at his son. He saw, in his Hyde Park cousin's instinctive grace, the "nobility of his spirit," and—for a moment that lodged forever in Nicholas's memory—the rift in the Roosevelt family disappeared as one clansman honored another. Franklin's buoyancy, forged in part by his determination to have everything at all times appear to go his way, was standing him in good stead.

As Franklin's pain began to lessen, the question of the most fitting future for him was often discussed. His doctor, George Draper, was struck by Franklin's courage and ambition but felt that his patient nonetheless had to be handled very carefully. The gravity of his condition should be revealed to him slowly and carefully, or "his extraordinarily sensitive emotional mechanism" could be crushed, forcing him into a small and circumscribed life. Sara believed that her son would be best served by just the small and circumscribed life his doctor feared.

Louis Howe marveled at Franklin's courage in those "black years," and he wanted to help him. He decided that the "greatest adventure" he could imagine would be "to put him in the White House."

Dynastic Struggle

ONCE AS A CHILD, Franklin had put on a cap to hide a deep cut
from his father. Now, as he tried to walk again, he masked his pain with
banter. He designed an exercise platform at Hyde Park with railings on the
sides, and as he pulled himself around it, he joked with friends who gathered on the lawn. He swung himself down the length of ten-foot parallel
bars and back, many times. He invented a traction frame to build up his
legs and an apparatus for hoisting himself out of bed. He crawled around
the floor of his room for hours, his lower body a dead weight, and over and
over again he pulled himself up the stairs of his house.

As Franklin's strength increased, he set about reclaiming his political life. He and Louis Howe and Eleanor plotted ways to keep the Roosevelt name alive for future campaigns. They decided to capitalize on the
fact that, for several years before Franklin's paralysis, Eleanor had pursued
her own political interests. Among other activities, she had served on the
first board of the League of Women Voters and had also begun to set up a
women's division within New York's Democratic Party. Seeing the political
benefit in organizing women voters, Eleanor and Franklin decided to place
a division vice chairwoman in each of New York's sixty-two counties.
Franklin drilled his wife thoroughly before every visit; he made sure that

she and her political friends knew the names of the key people in every county in the state. Eleanor's colleagues remembered Franklin fondly as a terrible taskmaster, because he quizzed them for hours after each trip. "We are doing some fine organizing work," Franklin said, "especially with the aid of the ladies." Each contact Eleanor made increased the exposure of the Franklin Roosevelt name.

But the sense of progress stopped abruptly when Franklin met with one of his doctors early in 1924 and was told it was unlikely he would ever again walk unaided. "I am very much disheartened about his ultimate recovery," George Draper told a colleague. Franklin left for Florida, where he drifted in a houseboat for ten weeks with friends. He spent each morning alone, until he had pulled himself together enough to laugh and talk as usual. By the time he reached home at the end of April, he had accepted the fact that his doctors could do nothing more.

Two months later, in New York City on June 26, 1924, pandemonium broke loose at the Democratic National Convention. An observer watched the crowd going "crazy" at the sight of Franklin Roosevelt entering Madison Square Garden. He had arrived, with one hand gripping his son James and the other gripping a crutch, to propose Alfred E. Smith for president. Weeks before, Franklin had marked off on his library floor at home the fifteen steps it would take for him to walk alone from his chair to the lectern. He had practiced for hour upon agonizing hour, struggling forward with each slow swing of his crutches.

Now, waiting his turn to speak, Franklin suddenly asked someone to test the speaker's stand to see if it would bear his weight. The least movement would throw him off balance, and he would fall like a stone before thousands of politicians and delegates. A friend knew that Franklin was frightened. His legs had no purchase in the rigid braces that ran from his hips to his feet.

Stiff-legged, Franklin leaned onto his forward crutch and began to drag himself slowly across the stage alone. At last he stood at the speaker's stand before the wildly cheering crowd. Friends sitting close by saw

Franklin trembling, but the confidence in his voice transformed his frail body. Alfred E. Smith was the " 'Happy Warrior' of the political battlefield," Franklin said—the one to make the "dry bones rattle" in Washington. One reporter called his nominating speech the best of the convention, with "less blah to the square inch." Years later, people would still speak of the light that poured down on Franklin that hot day, of the "glorious white figure" who had stood before them.

When he finished speaking, Franklin grasped the lectern more tightly with one hand, then let the other go. He raised it in a wave, daring to risk his balance—and his future—in the classic political gesture. The crowd roared. But then Franklin turned, awkwardly, from the stand, and Frances Perkins darted past politicians frozen in their seats to shield his fumbling with her skirt. From then on, women took care to stand near Franklin when he spoke, because dresses hid his crippled body better than men's suits.

After Franklin's speech, "song pluggers, Tammany shouters, Yiddish chanters, vaudeville performers . . . hula dancers [and] female stars of the silver screen"—as well as hundreds of jaded politicians—paraded around Madison Square Garden. One newspaper reported that Franklin's appearance incited the greatest demonstration that had ever been staged at a national convention. Smith's supporters commandeered baskets of cowbells, half a dozen fire sirens, and several ambulance alarm gongs, but the hour-long uproar was not for him. It was Franklin people were cheering, his name they wanted to place in nomination.

Minutes later, Franklin sat in a little room off the stage in the Garden, "shaking almost like a leaf," a friend said later. His gray and white suit was wringing wet, and he mopped his face as he laughed and chatted with political leaders. The temperature in the building registered ninety degrees, but Franklin also sweated from effort, tension, and fear. He knew the fifteen paces he had taken to the speaker's stand had restored him to political life. And he knew that ahead lay a thousand such journeys. He would have to be carried up countless flights of stairs, be lifted through fire escapes, and employ endless strategies to disguise the fact that he could barely move. Franklin wiped his brow and smiled up at the politicians, exhilarated but afraid.

THREE MONTHS LATER, on September 25, 1924, Ted Roosevelt was selected the Republican candidate for governor of New York State. His father had won the same nomination twenty-three years before. Ted's coming campaign unnerved him—and surprised Louis Howe; he had just told Franklin that "little Ted appears to be down and out as candidate for governor." A scandal had threatened Ted in 1921 when President Harding had appointed him to Franklin's—and Theodore's—office as assistant secretary of the Navy. Certain government-owned lands in Wyoming, called Teapot Dome, contained oil reserves for the exclusive use of the Navy, but a few companies had siphoned oil off illegally for private use. Ted had owned stock in one of the companies, although his wife had sold their shares well before the scandal erupted. He had helped expose the wrongdoing, and a Senate investigation had declared him innocent of complicity, but just the possibility of delinquent behavior was enough to contaminate a political race.

Despite Franklin's gallant effort, Alfred E. Smith had failed in his bid for the 1924 Democratic presidential nomination. On September 26, the day after Ted was chosen the Republican candidate for New York State governor, Smith was selected to run for reelection against him as the Democratic candidate. Eleanor gave the speech seconding his nomination. Would Smith win? she was asked. "How can he help it," Eleanor answered, "when even the Republican Convention yesterday did all that it could to help him?" Two thousand people rose to their feet and cheered Eleanor's attack on Ted. She had drawn the first blood of the campaign. A few minutes later, Eleanor spoke of Theodore's son again, damning him with faint praise. She called her first cousin a "personally nice young man whose pub-

Franklin with Alfred E. Smith, John W. Davis,
and George Lunn at Hyde Park in 1924

Eleanor, chair of the Women's
Advisory Committee, and Emily Blair,
vice chair of the Democratic National
Committee, in 1924

Eleanor with Louis Howe, seated opposite, and
others in Alfred E. Smith's New York governorship
campaign in 1924. Note teapots

Ted, who wanted a career in
the Army, was pressured into
becoming a politician.

lic service record shows him willing to do the bidding of his friends." The battle lines were set.

Colleagues were struck by Eleanor's political effectiveness. Frances Perkins noticed that she kept "three or four threads in mind at once" and did not hesitate to chastise local campaign committees. "You really must not just spend money carelessly," Eleanor told them. She was also quick to "telephone so-and-so and tell them why more money was needed." Eleanor made it clear in her autobiography that organizing was "primarily my job" in the campaign and that, with Louis Howe's help, she had thought up "some of the best stunts."

Together Eleanor and Howe had an enormous teapot built on the chassis of a car, which she parked wherever Ted spoke, reminding voters of his brush with the Teapot Dome affair. Later, Eleanor explained that they had resorted to the tactic because Howe had been waiting a long time "to get even" with Ted and his remark about Franklin's being a maverick. But Alice placed the blame on her cousin, saying that "it was a pretty base thing for her to do." Ted's wife claimed that Eleanor was the only one during the campaign to raise the sensitive Teapot Dome issue. Although Eleanor admitted that it had been "a rough stunt," it was also, as one knowledge-able observer put it, probably the only thing she ever did wrong. Even so, Eleanor's Long Island relatives never forgave her for the teapot car; there was still talk of it in Oyster Bay fifty years later.

In 1924, the cousins were competing against one another in ways they couldn't have imagined back in their childhood. The little girls had drawn close, sheltered within the bowl of light of Oyster Bay. But no longer. Many times, Eleanor drove the teapot car, noisily puffing steam from its spout, to the place where Ted was giving a campaign speech.

Her behavior reflected an allegiance to Franklin that swept aside all other considerations. Helen Robinson wrote Bye that she dreaded the thought of Christmas in Hyde Park with Eleanor and Franklin. She com-plained that Eleanor had become politically "rabid," and that her husband, Teddy, scarcely spoke to Franklin. Yet Helen knew the cousins must con-tinue to spend holidays together. If they didn't, even the civilities among them would cease. Helen's dilemma was emblematic of how deeply the dissension was affecting the relationships among the Roosevelt women. Corinne Jr. had admired Eleanor since they were children, and in the years to come she would recall the satisfying talks they had as teenagers. But after 1924, although she and her cousin continued to see each other on holidays from time to time, and exchanged fond notes on family matters, true intimacy was a thing of the past. Corinne Jr.'s thirteen-year-old granddaughter, Elizabeth Alsop, would not realize until Eleanor's death that she had been her grandniece. She had never even met her.

In the fall of 1924, Corinne Jr. was campaigning for a seat in the Connecticut State Assembly. In her village of Avon on election night, the townsfolk would parade through her house, banging on pots and pans, to celebrate her victory; but within the family, Corinne Jr.'s campaign was eclipsed by the drama played out between the Oyster Bay Roosevelts and the Hyde Park Roosevelts in the New York governorship race. While Eleanor campaigned vigorously against Ted, Alice was acting informally—and effectively—as his manager. Whenever they were both in Washington, she and Ted were likely to be in and out of each other's houses several times a day—for lunch, a poker game, a dinner party. The topic was nearly always politics. Once Alice had read the pages of her father's speeches as fast as he had written them; now she read her brother's.

Alice was considered a leading political figure in her own right, despite the fact that Nick was speaker of the House. Her name, Corinne Jr. said, "meant power in the 1920's." Certainly Alice's political potential did not escape her, for she was often asked to run for some office or another. "If we must have a Roosevelt," one newspaper wrote, "let it be Alice." But she always said no, probably because she had not been raised to wield power on her own behalf. Instead, Alice claimed to prefer smoky backroom deals and gossip about the strange bedfellows politics made. She relished the stories of President Harding's philandering under his wife's nose in the public spaces in the White House—on top of desks and in small closets near the Oval Office. "My God," she said, "we have a President of the United States who doesn't even know *beds* were invented."

Alice had assumed the leadership of Theodore's supporters on his death, and she had won their loyalty during the struggle to defeat the League of Nations. Now she called on the Roosevelt loyalists to champion her brother's candidacy for the governorship. "Give them the bayonet, Teddy! Ram her home, God bless you!" people wrote Ted. Letters arrived at his headquarters calling up images of Theodore: "Hit him hard like your *daddy* would." They were determined to find in the son a replica of the father. If Ted had not already had similarities to Theodore, one columnist observed, his supporters would have "compelled them" in him. But the comparisons sometimes wounded. "I would give the world," one letter went, "if we only had your father back again." A reporter claimed to see Ted's facial muscles twitch when Theodore was mentioned; he thought it was difficult for him to "keep back the tears." Pressured from all sides by his family's love and ambition, Ted tried on his old Army uniform one morning and confessed, "I loved getting into it. I wanted to strut up and down."

By the end of 1924, three Roosevelt cousins had followed one another into positions once held by Theodore. Franklin, Teddy Robinson, and Ted had sat on the New York State legislature; Franklin and Ted had served as assistant secretary of the Navy, while Teddy Robinson was appointed to the post when Ted resigned in 1924. But with the New York State governorship, the family pattern changed decisively. Teddy Robinson never ran for governor and died in 1934 at the age of fifty-one. Ted put up a strong fight for the office, but he lost the election and never waged another political campaign. The Roosevelt path was clear for Franklin, who had already swung fifteen steps down it that summer. In 1928 he was elected governor of New York.

When Franklin's daughter, Anna, looking back years later, said that in "Father's fight with young TR, there was more than politics," she was hinting at a truth the Greek playwrights had long known. In order to heighten dramatic tension, they set their tragedies within families, where tears are mixed with blood.

Epilogue

ON OCTOBER 31, 1932, in a New York City taxicab, newswoman Lorena Hickok turned to her friend Eleanor and asked her if she knew what Edith Roosevelt had just done. Theodore's widow was reclusive and walked alone over the fields of Sagamore Hill in all weathers—like a gypsy, she told her son Ted. But earlier that evening Edith had come out of her seclusion and driven to a political rally at Madison Square Garden. Dressed all in black, her pale face burning in the spotlight, she had raised black-gloved hands and asked the wildly cheering crowd to vote for Herbert Hoover, the Republican candidate for president.

Edith had not agreed with Ted when he told her Franklin was "such poor stuff" he wouldn't be elected president. All summer, letters had arrived at Sagamore Hill addressed to her and full of praise for the Democratic presidential candidate who they believed was Theodore's son. Edith blamed Franklin for capitalizing on that belief, and she blamed him for Ted's failed political career. She did not want Franklin to be elected president. At Madison Square Garden, she offered up the memory of her dead husband in an attempt to defeat him.

Her effort failed. On November 8, two Secret Service agents in dark suits slipped into a room at the Democratic Headquarters in New York's

Biltmore Hotel. Word had just come that Franklin, the governor of New York State, had won the presidential election.

Four months later, when the Roosevelts gathered in the White House on the evening of Franklin's inauguration, their ranks were noticeably thin. Ted was at his new post as governor-general of the Philippines, and Nick Longworth had died of pneumonia in 1931, in the Aiken, South Carolina, house of someone rumored to be his lover. There were other conspicuous absences, among them Edith. Her husband had mentored two political sons, but on March 4, 1933, no victory of Ted's was celebrated in the White House, and that night no one spoke Theodore's name.

Some of the Roosevelts deliberately deepened the schism that was an unwitting part of Theodore's legacy. Even though they knew he would have been saddened by a rupture in the family, they continued to widen the breach out of allegiance to Ted and jealousy of Franklin. When a reporter asked Edith one day why Kermit had paid a visit to Franklin, she snapped that it was because she—his mother—hadn't been there. Her blond son, Edith said, was "the one with the white head and the black heart." Alice claimed to have been tempted to join Franklin at his political rallies, until she realized it would be construed as disloyalty to Ted. "I really could have had a lot of fun with Franklin if only the damned old presidency hadn't come between us," she said. "There was this family feeling which I didn't brood about, but which was definitely there." Instead, she had written articles supporting Herbert Hoover and had traveled with him on one of his campaign swings.

People curious about the new president began to ask his relatives what Franklin had been like as a boy. One Oyster Bay cousin elected to remember that when they were children, Franklin had reminded them of the dainty porcelain man who pirouetted on the top of their handkerchief boxes. Not effeminate, another cousin added, but not rugged, either. The Oyster Bay Roosevelts were inclined, too, to talk about Eleanor's grim childhood and not about her graceful years at Allenswood. They went so far as to describe the First Lady with the condescending phrase they had applied so often to Elliott's orphaned young daughter: "Poor little Eleanor,"

Corinne Jr. said to Frances Perkins as they stood together in the White House. "I remember her in the old days." It had always angered Alice that people thought Eleanor was more Theodore's daughter—more like him—than she was. Her new prominence made it worse, and Alice's response was to protrude her upper lip and voice banal opinions in a merciless impersonation of her cousin. "Nobody," Nicholas von Hoffman observed, "got Alice as frantically jealous as did Eleanor."

In 1933, the country was at the bottom of the Great Depression, and one of Franklin's first acts as president was to press for legislation to provide work for the unemployed. Even though many people thought his New Deal plan implemented Theodore's 1912 Progressive Party platform, Alice ridiculed Franklin publicly. In 1936, in a newspaper column headlined HIS MOLLYCODDLE PHILOSOPHY IS CALLED TYPICAL OF ROOSEVELT, she contrasted what she referred to as Franklin's philosophy of security and dependency with her father's belief in the strenuous life. Alice wrote that Theodore, who had conquered his childhood disabilities, had passed on to the nation the Spartan virtues of toughness and self-discipline. She maintained that Franklin, on the other hand, because he had adapted to his illness, was encouraging the country to live with the Depression rather than overcome it.

Eleanor, in her syndicated column, "My Day," defended Franklin against Alice's attack. "No man who has brought himself back from what might have been an entire life of invalidism," she wrote, "can ever be accused of preaching or exemplifying a mollycoddle philosophy." Undeterred, Alice mounted yet another, more destructive assault on Franklin when America faced the reality of the Second World War. The president believed the country should fight if necessary, but a group called America First, of which Alice was a prominent member, had taken the opposite stance. Alice's rationale was that since her father had opposed the League of Nations and further involvement in European affairs in 1919, twenty years later he would have opposed the presence of American forces on the European continent.

But the powerful America First organization, for Alice, was really just another weapon with which to fight Franklin, because the movement opposed him as vigorously as it resisted entry into the war. As she had during Franklin's 1920 vice-presidential campaign and their fight over the League of Nations, Alice, unconscionably, treated affairs of state as if they were moves in a chess game she was playing with her cousin. Later, she admitted that her activities had been made "entirely of mischief and dislike of Franklin. Anything," she said, "to annoy Franklin."

Alice had been worse than mischievous. Her actions had been reprehensible, threatening the nation's security for personal ends. Franklin refused, finally, to allow "that damned woman" into the White House again.

LATE ONE NIGHT in her White House sitting room, Eleanor sat working at her desk when Hall's daughter, also named Eleanor, came to her and asked if there were ghosts about. "Oh, yes, sure," she replied calmly. "There are people here." Nearly every night, usually around midnight, Eleanor told her niece, she would look up from her desk because she was sure someone had just come into the room.

There was no more considerable ghost than Theodore. And no more telling moment as to how far Eleanor and Franklin had traveled from Oyster Bay than when she incurred her husband's anger by speaking fondly of her uncle to a visitor. The publisher Fulton Oursler was moved by the warmth of Eleanor's recollections and asked her to write about Theodore. She accepted, but a few days later he received a note of refusal. Under the circumstances, Eleanor wrote, she felt it would be "in bad taste."

By 1932, several Roosevelts had stepped forward from the frieze of cousins and played out their fates in relation to Theodore. Some, Eleanor, Ted, and Teddy Robinson among them, had wanted to please him, and had tried to emulate his example. Others, with Alice in the lead, wanted to canonize his memory. A few—and Franklin was one of these—wanted to surpass him. In the cousins' doing was the undoing of a family, for, without realizing it, Theodore had placed them on a collision course: They could not succeed without competing with one another. Decades later, Alice praised the Kennedy family for being "all for one and one for all" and criticized her own relatives for being "completely individualistic." She complained that the Roosevelts were not a family that "hung together." Yet the cousins knew that, deep as Theodore's desire had been for a united Roosevelt clan, he had also fought all his life for the dignity of the individual. He would not have wanted them to sacrifice their separate dreams.

Sometimes the cousins were able to embrace the haunting paradox Theodore had embodied. They managed—at moments—to honor their clan and their individual differences at the same time.

Ted, like Alice, had been involved with the America First movement, but finally he dissociated himself from their pacifism. In April 1941, he rejoined his old regiment, the 26th Infantry, and cheered his men on during heavy fighting by reciting poems Theodore had taught him as a boy. Ted had not felt like his father's son during his political travails. But when he returned to soldiering, as Theodore had tried to do in World War I, it was, one of Ted's nephews said, an "emotional homecoming." Franklin raised Ted's rank to brigadier general, and Ted thought his cousin wanted to show the public that "the hatchet" had been buried.

Arthritic, stumping along, fifty-seven-year-old Ted was the oldest soldier on Normandy Beach on D day. When General Omar Bradley was later asked the most heroic moment in wartime, he recalled Brigadier General Roosevelt, propped up on his cane to make himself visible to his men, heedless of the fact that he had made himself visible to the Germans as well. Ted died in France of a heart attack in 1944, and one of his sons cabled home the news in the same words used to announce Theodore's death twenty-five years before: "The old lion is dead." Franklin awarded Ted, posthumously, the Congressional Medal of Honor.

When Ted's brother Archie came back from the war, he paid a visit to Franklin in the White House. Noticing a crumpled cigarette pack on his cousin's desk in the Oval Office, Archie pressed into Franklin's hand his own dented metal cigarette case, carried through seventy-six straight days

Franklin and Eleanor (seated, center) sailing with family and friends from Massachusetts to Campobello in 1933

Brigadier General Ted Roosevelt in Europe during World War II

Eleanor and Franklin relaxing on the lawn in Hyde Park in 1933

Alice Roosevelt Longworth as an old woman

of combat during the Pacific campaign. Franklin was moved. He felt Archie's gift from the battlefield was a silent salute to him as a kinsman in arms. But Franklin did not keep the case. Knowing what the memento would mean to Archie's wife, Grace, he sent it on to her, and asked her not to tell his cousin.

Archie was proud that his family presented a united front during the war. "Regardless of the bitterness that many people feel toward the 'Hyde Park' Roosevelts or the 'Oyster Bay' Roosevelts," he wrote Franklin, "they have to admit that the whole clan has turned out to a man." All of Franklin's sons saw action. Under gunfire during an air attack aboard a naval ship, Franklin Jr. carried a soldier, his leg shot off, to the sick bay; James's commando unit saw such heavy fighting that one of its raids was chronicled in a war movie; John received the Bronze Star; at one point Elliott's unit was losing twenty planes a week. With so many Roosevelt men on the front lines, the war seemed to some people infused as much with Theodore's fighting spirit as with Franklin's.

Although Franklin embraced the signs of reconciliation with his Oyster Bay relatives, he did not become, within the family, the leader Theodore had been. Eleanor and his sons said Sara's interference in his life had made Franklin wary of guiding relatives even in small ways. He remained genial and supportive, but helped only when asked. The country seemed sympathetic to Franklin's attitude, for across America rigid family hierarchies were giving way to looser, more egalitarian structurings. Nicholas, trailing at the end of a generation of Roosevelts, recollected the communal campfire his older cousins liked to describe, but in his day, each young Roosevelt made his own fire and cooked his own steak.

Franklin had no wish to be a patriarch, but, like Theodore, he encouraged both family unity and independence. He supported Eleanor's political initiative as she fought for the wounded and the disenfranchised. Better than anyone, Franklin knew his wife could not, as she put it, "take my place in a warm corner by the fireside and simply look on." Louis Howe knew it too. One day he came into Eleanor's White House sitting room and curled up, shrewd and gnomelike, on the sofa. He told her that if she wanted to be president in 1940, "tell me now so I can start getting things ready."

But while Franklin respected Eleanor's independence, he also wished they could be closer companions. One of his sons said that Franklin, increasingly frail under the terrible stress of the war years, played up his frailties at times in order to try to keep Eleanor near him. And he had plans to take her with him, when the war ended, to Saudi Arabia, where together they would find ways to irrigate the desert. He and Eleanor could do a "magnificent job" out there, Franklin told Frances Perkins a few months before his death. When Elliott reported to his mother that Franklin hoped they could "learn to know each other again," he says Eleanor told him she hoped so, too.

But Eleanor could not forget her pain over Franklin's love affair. Many years later, a relative saw her "stiffen" when a conversation veered dangerously near the name of Lucy Mercer. She remained too deeply hurt—"too busy"—to dare approach her former intimacy with Franklin. Instead, Eleanor found portions of closeness in friendships with women and with other men. Some of her biographers would speculate later over the extent to which those relationships had contained a physical dimension. They were encouraged to do so by the words Eleanor used. The language of the Victorians was ornate, sentimental in ways we today find foreign and, often innocently, suggestive. Lorena Hickok writes of wanting to kiss her friend Eleanor at "the corner of your mouth"; Eleanor, in a letter to "Hick," refers to "looking at your picture & kissing it goodnight." It is not possible to know if they meant anything by this effulgence beyond a very affectionate friendship. At least one friend, herself a lesbian, judged Eleanor not to be one. "I never heard her express herself on homosexuals," Esther Lape said. "She couldn't bring herself to consider that."

Several men were also thought to be Eleanor's lovers, among them Earl Miller, a former state trooper Franklin hired to be her bodyguard. Miller brought out Eleanor's playful side, and there is a picture of her sitting comfortably at a picnic with friends, her hand resting casually on his thigh. History has no reason to exclude Eleanor, out of prudery, from the pleasures of physical intimacy, but neither has it evidence enough to establish anyone, male or female, as her lover.

Regardless of the nature of Eleanor's friendships, they and her work largely filled her life. "I could have her with me so much more if she didn't have so many other engagements," Franklin complained to their son Elliott. He turned again to his married friend Lucy Mercer Rutherfurd. By then, one of Franklin's sons believed, what physical passion there had—or hadn't—been was a thing of the past. Franklin and Lucy saw each other from time to time, secure in their old love. On April 12, 1945, they were in Warm Springs, Georgia, laughing and talking with friends while his portrait was being painted, when suddenly he put his hand on his forehead and complained of a headache. That day, when Franklin died of a cerebral hemorrhage, Lucy's presence no doubt seemed to Eleanor like betrayal. A double betrayal, in fact, because she also learned that sometimes when she had been away, her daughter Anna had arranged, at Franklin's request, for Lucy to dine with him in the White House. But Eleanor was aware that Lucy's presence when Franklin died—"what happened at Warm Springs," as she put it—was the result of a failure in which she had played a role. "I have thought very hard about that," she told her son Elliott. "I can only blame my own pigheadedness, not Father . . . It was really my responsibility."

"And Lucy Rutherfurd?" Elliott asked.

"She deserves forgiveness as much as anyone," Eleanor said, and when her son turned to a lighter topic, she interrupted him suddenly: "If only I had found the *courage* to talk to Franklin as I wanted to." She told Elliott that she wished she had said, "Let us bury this whole matter and begin over again together." But she had not, and although her son maintained that "the fault lay elsewhere," it also seemed that Eleanor had conquered every fear except one—the fear of being rejected, as she had felt rejected as a child.

(The mirror image of Eleanor's fear could be found in Alice in 1951, although she compensated for it differently: According to the psychiatrist Lawrence S. Kubie, Alice was "enslaved to her father's memory to a degree that I have never seen equalled." He wrote Eleanor that Alice "literally carries around with her a 10,000 page encyclopedia from his speeches and writings.")

After Franklin's death, it became clear how deeply Eleanor understood the distant Hyde Park cousin who had been her husband for nearly forty years. She wrote that although Franklin might have been "happier with a wife who was completely uncritical," she was incapable of that kind of love, so "he had to find it in some other people." Eleanor knew that her husband "was particularly attracted to women," but she also knew his flirtations had likely remained just that. "You must come right back and get rid of her," Franklin would call Eleanor to complain of a visitor. "This is getting out of hand!"

"He could afford to indulge in this weakness," Eleanor said, "for I always responded to the summons."

But some of Franklin's friendships had been more serious. He had been close to his secretary Missy Lehand, and dependent on her in ways someone in a wheelchair must always be. "Franklin loved Missy," Eleanor told a friend. "He couldn't have lived without me, but neither could he have lived without Missy. She became fine and he was fine, so it was all right. If he had met her earlier, it would have been different."

No one had lived with graver responsibilities than Franklin. Eleanor felt that if a man used himself fully, he was worthy of love and worthy of the sacrifices made for him. There were, she wrote, "no regrets." Each January 30, Franklin's birthday, Eleanor put on the old tweed coat he had worn at Harvard and stood for some moments, her head bowed, before his grave in the Hyde Park rose garden. Then she knelt and laid out dozens of flowers and carefully wove them, one by one, into an intricate and colorful pattern in the ivy that covered her husband's grave. Her private ritual was testimony to a poem found on her nightstand when she died in 1962. "The soul that had believed / And was deceived," the last lines read, "Ends by believing / More than ever before."

By the 1940s, a half century lay between the cousins' shared childhood, when sunlight had glanced off Oyster Bay, and the present, when flashbulbs ceaselessly recorded their separate lives. At times even Eleanor and Alice succeeded in reconciling the two images. Like Archie, Ted, and Franklin during the war, they celebrated family loyalty while saluting their differences. Finding themselves on a train together one day, Eleanor and Alice fell into easy talk about their family, just as they had when they were young. Eleanor was struck by her cousin's comment that no matter how much they differed politically, there was still a "tribal feeling" between them. Given the bad temper Alice usually displayed toward Eleanor and Franklin, her remark seemed comically specious. Yet Eleanor herself was quick to tell a reporter that "if real trouble came," she and her cousin might make "good allies." After all, she added, "Fundamental Roosevelt characteristics gravitate towards each other in times of stress!"

Eleanor told a friend later that she found Alice "a vivid & amusing creature no matter how unkind at times." Despite the bitter years, she remained loyal to her cousin. Lawrence Kubie, in his 1951 letter to Eleanor, fired off a volley of sharp judgments about Alice, among them that she had "sold her birthright for a wise-crack," that she was "tormented by her envy of the Hyde Park Roosevelts, and especially of you," and that "she likes only people who are not 'good.'" Eleanor deflected the harsh criticisms by replying simply, "Alice always makes me sad because I like her very much." In turn, Alice was capable, briefly, of the same defense of her cousin. She once reprimanded an interviewer sharply when he started to repeat Edith's much-quoted remark about Eleanor as a little girl, that the gawky "ugly duckling" might turn out to be—"Not a swan," Alice interrupted angrily. "Something much better than a swan," and her words freed Eleanor from the Oyster Bay condescension for all time.

Alice remained in Washington, an unruly presence on the political scene, long after Franklin and Eleanor died. Presidents asked her to dine, and her invitations to tea were coveted, for Alice's sharp-tongued wit was admired, but sometimes, as she neared death in 1980, Alice would look around, confused, and ask, was Eleanor still alive?

The following abbreviations have been used throughout the notes:

P E O P L E

ARC	Anna Roosevelt Cowles (Bye)
ARL	Alice Roosevelt Longworth
CRA	Corinne Robinson Alsop (Corinne Jr.)
CRR	Corinne Roosevelt Robinson
ER	Eleanor Roosevelt
FDR	Franklin Delano Roosevelt
HRR	Helen Roosevelt Robinson
SDR	Sara Delano Roosevelt
TR	Theodore Roosevelt
TR Jr.	Theodore Roosevelt Jr.

I N S T I T U T I O N S A N D C O L L E C T I O N S

Columbia U. OH	Columbia University Oral History Research Office Collection, New York City, New York
FDRL	Franklin Delano Roosevelt Library, Hyde Park, New York
MDLC	Manuscript Division Library of Congress, Washington, D.C.
TRCH	Theodore Roosevelt Collection, Houghton Library at Harvard University, Cambridge, Massachusetts

Prologue

Details concerning city life come from the following newspapers during December 1902: the *NY Post, The World* (New York), *The Sun* (New York), the *NY Herald,* the *NY Times,* and the *Mail and Express* (New York); and from the society magazines *Town Topics* and *Town and Country.* Alice's activities are drawn from her diary entries for the same month.

4   *in a yellow dress: Town and Country,* 6/27/03
      in gales of laughter: HRR to ARC, 6/11/00, TRCH
      "madly gay": CRR to CRA, 1/20/03, TRCH
      let her green pet snake: Teague, p. 69
      How she smoked: Kermit Roosevelt to ARL, n.d., ARL Papers, MDLC
      "second establishment": ARL diary 6/11/03, ARL Papers, MDLC
      "Wait until I am": ARL diary, 3/8/03, ARL Papers, MDLC
      sometimes he escaped: Eleanor Roosevelt, *Your Teens and Mine,* p. 81
      brandishing a pistol: CRA unpublished memoirs, copy in possession of Elizabeth
          Winthrop
6   *"entire situation":* Eleanor Roosevelt, *This Is My Story,* p. 99
      "a little afraid": ibid., p. 16
      "poor Eleanor": Teague, p. 151
      Four days later: FDR journal, 12/9/02, Roosevelt Family Business and Personal Papers,
          FDRL
7   *She wrote later: This Is My Story,* pp. 51, 100
9   *"personified" . . . "to the fifth degree":* Nicholas Roosevelt, p. 20
      A newspaper reported: Mail and Express, 12/10/02
      when asked in interviews: ARL, interview by Joseph Lash, 2/6/67, Joseph P. Lash
          Papers, FDRL
      and remembered calling: Teague, p. 156
      a friend remembered her: Susan Hammond, interview, 1/19/67, Lash Papers, FDRL

PART ONE

YOUNG COUSINS

1882–1902

Theodore

The events in Theodore's life during this period can be found in greater detail in Henry Pringle's *Theodore Roosevelt,* David McCullough's *Mornings on Horseback,* and Edmund Morris's *The Rise of Theodore Roosevelt.*

13   *His older sister, Anna:* Hagedorn notes, Hermann Hagedorn Papers, TRCH
      the rhythmic tread: Edmund Morris, p. 143
      held his infant daughter: Anna Bulloch Gracie diary, 3/25/84, TRCH
      Alice Hathaway Lee: Monk, p. 23
14   *secret understanding:* William Merrifield, interview by Hermann Hagedorn, 6/1919,
          Carlton Putnam Papers, TRCH
      It was rumored: Amory, p. 317
      "I did not think": Edmund Morris, p. 121
      "They are both": Anna Gracie Bulloch to CRR, 8/5/83, TRCH

like "Hell": "Roosevelt in the Badlands" by Alvar W. Carlson in *Journal of the West*,
10/19/70, p. 473

courted every challenge: Hagedorn Badlands notes and unattributed press clippings,
Carlton Putnam Papers, TRCH

A friend said: ibid.

17 *"much at home":* TR, *An Autobiography,* p. 29

"sheer industry": ibid., p. 34

inspired by the story: ibid., p. 54

"By acting as if": ibid.

William Sewall remembered: Hagedorn Badlands notes, Hermann Hagedorn Papers,
TRCH

"Her aunt can take": Sewall, p. 47

The young widower seemed: Hagedorn Badlands notes and unattributed press clippings,
Carlton Putnam Papers, TRCH

"all teeth and eyes": Hagedorn Badlands notes and unattributed press clippings, Carlton Putman Papers, TRCH

the Roosevelts were . . . "They had no business": Hagedorn, *Roosevelt in the Badlands,*
p. 241

"You surely won't" . . . "going across": ibid., p. 250

18 *"the man who":* Hagedorn Badlands notes, Hermann Hagedorn Papers, TRCH

In the years to come: Roosevelt in the Badlands, p. 466

Before he went: Hagedorn Badlands notes, Hermann Hagedorn Papers, TRCH

Alice and Eleanor

19 *Shortly before his arrival:* Anna Bulloch Gracie diary, 6/24/85, TRCH

Years later, Theodore: TR to ARC, 9/20/86, TRCH

a story she wrote: in CRR handwritten notebooks, "Book VII," 11/25/76; "Book VIII,"
12/2/76, TRCH

21 *Theodore had taken:* William Merrifield, interview by Hermann Hagedorn, 6/1919,
Carlton Putnam Papers, TRCH

"too good and happy": TR to ARC, 7/1/88, TRCH

He told his younger sister: TR to CRR, 8/14/87, TRCH

22 *his daughter bore the brunt:* Teague, p. 13

Her aunts worried: CRR to ARC, 8/17/89, TRCH

"quiet and mousy": Hagedorn, *Sagamore Hill,* p. 24

He teasingly called her: TR to ARC, 7/1/88, TRCH

"little white penguin": Sagamore Hill, p. 16

"Saying good-bye": Longworth, p. 21

24 *Anna had a flawless:* Lash, *Eleanor and Franklin,* p. 23

"the shadow of ": Olin Dows, interview by Emily Williams, 7/7/78, ER Oral History
Project, FDRL

Eight young Astor: Brandt, pp. 214–15

Late at night: ibid., p. 228

25 *and waited to see:* James Roosevelt, My Parents, p. 10

Elliott Roosevelt had been: Lash, Love, Eleanor, p. 5

"I woke up with": Anna Hall Roosevelt to Nannie Roosevelt, n.d., TRCH

"I never doubted": Eleanor Roosevelt, *This Is My Story,* p. 9

25 *On May 18:* NY Times, 5/23/87
Eleanor dangled: This Is My Story, p. 7
"one unknown leg": NY Times, 5/23/87
27 *Nicholas later remembered:* Nicholas Roosevelt, p. 21
Years later, Eleanor: This Is My Story, pp. 5–6
"She has such": Anna Bulloch Gracie to CRR, 6/6 (no year), TRCH
Anna would write: Eleanor and Franklin, p. 31
A family member noted: ibid.
28 *Alice even shared:* ibid., p. 72
even at a young age: Teague, p. 151
Years later, Nicholas: Nicholas Roosevelt, p. 21
the sight of the girl's: Anna Bulloch Gracie to CRR 5/14 (no year), TRCH

River Families

29 *"Welcome back":* SDR to Warren and Jennie Delano circa 1907, Roosevelt Family
  Papers, FDRL
laughing at: SDR diary, 11/11/82, Roosevelt Family Papers, FDRL
When he was a small: SDR, p. 11
30 *Franklin was happy . . . would be like his:* Kleeman, *Young Franklin Roosevelt*, p. 15
often stopped by the village: Ward, *Before the Trumpet*, p. 142
Eleanor praised the: ER, *My Day*, vol. 1, p. 76
Examples given by Eleanor: Young Franklin Roosevelt, p. 119
when Franklin asked: ibid., pp. 90–91
On another occasion: ibid., pp. 80–81
he accompanied James: Before the Trumpet, p. 148
32 *on ice that rose and fell:* Honoria McVitty, interview by Emily Williams, 10/16/78, ER
  Oral History Project, FDRL
People often raced: Dows, p. 59
His "virile, blood-curdling": SDR, p. 30
Franklin's cousin: Laura Delano, interview by Joseph P. Lash, 6/25 (no year), Joseph
  P. Lash Papers, FDRL
Years later, Eleanor agreed: ER, *This I Remember*, p. 16
his great-grandmother: Young Franklin Roosevelt, p. 45
"Oh for freedom": ibid., pp. 119–20
James, in a discussion: Lash, *Eleanor and Franklin*, p. 117
33 *Each time a carriage:* Dows, p. 31
Years later, he sat: Elliott Roosevelt, *Rendezvous with Destiny*, p. 45
a friend recalled: Helen Cutting Wilmerding, interview, 4/29/66, Lash Papers, FDRL
35 *"I became very self-conscious":* ER, *Your Teens and Mine*, p. 20
the "old-fashioned" child: ER, *This Is My Story*, pp. 17–18
Eleanor once confessed: Levy and Russett, p. 142
A lifelong friend found: Three Friends, "In Loving Memory of Anna Hall Roosevelt,"
  p. 7, privately printed memoir, Roosevelt Family Papers, Donated by the children,
  FDRL
She wrote that Anne Frank: ER, *My Day*, vol. 3, p. 75
36 *They knelt together:* "In Loving Memory," p. 33, Roosevelt Family Papers, Donated by
  the children, FDRL

"I must *know*": ibid., p. 27

in describing her childhood: This Is My Story, p. 28

Franklin and Eleanor once: Helen Gahagan Douglas, interview by Emily Williams, 1/22/79, ER Oral History, FDRL

There is a story: My Day, vol. 1, p. 137

According to one of their sons: James Roosevelt, *My Parents,* p. 179

Archibald MacLeish . . . "by a touch": MacLeish, pp. 1–2

37 *At the end:* Your Teens and Mine, p. 29

"still small" . . . "not conscious": ibid.

"painfully, step by step": ER, You Learn by Living, p. 25

"I learned to stare": ibid.

"with each victory": Your Teens and Mine, pp. 29–30

Years later, her cousin Alice: ARL, interview, 4/5/66, Lash Papers, FDRL

38 *Some of Franklin's biographers:* Miller, p. 19; Gosnell, p. 14; Ward, *Before the Trumpet,* p. 139

a friend remembered Franklin: Margaret Dix Lawrence, interview, 2/18/67, Lash Papers, FDRL

he went there: Dows, p. 54

A neighbor described Franklin: Olin Dows, interview by Emily Williams, 8/8/78, ER Oral History Project, FDRL

"where all the fun was": Margaret Dix Lawrence, interview, 2/18/67, Lash Papers, FDRL

The children dressed: Brandt, p. 223

"All through the autumn weeks": My Day, vol. 1, pp. 169–70

"Dances during the": ibid.

40 *Margaret Dix remembered:* Margaret Dix Lawrence, interview, 1/14/67, Lash Papers, FDRL

Fourth of July in Oyster Bay

41 *Eleanor loved the sentimental:* ER, Your Teens and Mine, p. 117

"going to live": Reminiscences of Frances Perkins, vol. 3, pt. 4, p. 535, Columbia U. OH

42 *"so polite":* ibid., p. 540

"charming, vigorous, bright": ibid., p. 542

in her dark blue smock: Margaret Dix Lawrence, interview by Joseph P. Lash, 1/14/67, Joseph P. Lash Papers, FDRL

into a thick pigtail: Emily de la Grange, interview, 1/12/67, Lash Papers, FDRL

They thought: Helen Cutting Wilmerding, interview, 4/29/66, Lash Papers, FDRL

What struck Helen: ibid.

"hard-minded": Teague, p. 18

44 *Alice's piano teacher:* Brough, p. 77

"I didn't do any of": Teague, p. 154

"always made a": ibid.

"selfish and defiant": ibid.

Later, Alice said: ibid., p. 18

"I am so glad": Lash, Love, Eleanor, p. 24

Eleanor was no longer: ER, This Is My Story, p. 35

Alice, Ted, and Franklin: Kleeman, Young Franklin Roosevelt, p. 103

45 *"I never wished":* Cook, p. 92

Nicholas's belief: Nicholas Roosevelt, p. 20

favorite niece: Love, Eleanor, p. 127

"Please don't make": Lash, *Eleanor and Franklin,* p. 118

"for as long as": TR to FDR, 6/11/97, Roosevelt Family Papers, FDRL

Franklin wrote his mother: Ward, *Before the Trumpet,* p. 194

"in trade": Anna Halstead, interview, 6/22/66, Lash Papers, FDRL

"nocturnal rambles": Teague, p. 51

47 *"It is an excellent":* TR, *An Autobiography,* p. 174

His eldest son, Ted: TR Jr. unattributed news clipping, 1/23/24, TR Jr. Papers, MDLC

Alice would not: Longworth, p. 1

Sometimes they ate: TR Jr., *All in the Family,* p. 22–3

Theodore's "tribal affection": ARL, interview, 4/5/66, Lash Papers, FDRL

His niece Corinne: CRA unpublished memoir, copy in possession of Elizabeth Winthrop

More than forty years later: Complete Presidential Press Conferences, #540, FDRL

48 *"desperately afraid": This Is My Story,* p. 50

"rather chunky": Longworth, p. 17

"Oh, those perfectly awful": Teague, p. 42

"My cousin Eleanor": ibid.

On Campobello he: ER, *My Day,* vol. 3, p. 315

His behavior was unaffected: Hagedorn, *Sagamore Hill,* p. 34

Theodore's thesis at Harvard: Collier with Horowitz, p. 53

49 *"black care":* TR, *"Ranch Life" in Works* vol. 1, p. 329

"I think I must": ER, *Autobiography,* p. 428

writing about happiness: TR, *An Autobiography,* p. 365

Eleanor would write that: ER, "In Pursuit of Happiness" in *Woman's Journal,* 8/47, p. 20

Sometimes he paused: Your Teens and Mine, p. 121

"whose admiration": ibid., p. 33

A friend said later: Perkins, vol. 3, pt. 1, p. 71, Columbia U. OH

On the Fourth of July: Sagamore Hill, pp. 83–5

Fourteen-Year-Olds

The description of Franklin's years at Groton, except where otherwise noted, is drawn from Geoffrey Ward's *Before the Trumpet.*

51 *he took the red Santa:* Dows, p. 60

he wrote about: Ward, *Before the Trumpet,* p. 202

52 *thought everybody:* Peabody to Harrison, 12/19/32, Endicott Peabody Papers, TRCH

memories of younger students: Before the Trumpet, pp. 202–3

But in 1909: Peabody to Acheson, 3/13/09, Peabody Papers, TRCH

Peabody did not find: Peabody to Harrison, 12/19/32, Peabody Papers, TRCH

"If a man has courage": Collier with Horowitz, p. 109

53 *"If some Groton boys":* Lash, *Eleanor and Franklin,* p. 117

when he strode: Town Topics, 1/29/03

Franklin studied: Kleeman, *Young Franklin Roosevelt,* p. 143
Franklin was known: Lindley, p. 53
There was no excuse: Eleanor and Franklin, p. 119

55 *Bye gave the girls:* ARL to ARC, 12/27/94; ER to ARC, 12/27/94, TRCH
"more pain": ER, *This Is My Story,* p. 51
"She made a": Teague, p. 154
"I knew, of course": This Is My Story, p. 51
"She claimed": Teague, p. 154
"I felt, as only": ER, *The Autobiography of Eleanor Roosevelt,* p. 411
"She was always": Teague, p. 154
"Of his own volition": ER, *Your Teens and Mine,* p. 25

56 *Franklin had told his mother:* ibid., p. 180
By the age of fourteen: ibid., p. 119
Ambition struck . . . Eleanor praised: Eleanor and Franklin, p. 69
"suffered from being": Teague, p. 154
"to wipe out completely": CRA unpublished memoir, copy in possession of Elizabeth
   Winthrop
"I don't think": Teague, p. 5
One photograph . . . Theodore's favorite: ibid., p. 6

57 *"I will never see her":* ER diary, 11/18/98, ER Papers, FDRL
"I hope I shall": ER to ARL, n.d., ARL Papers, MDLC
It was the sort: ER, *This Is My Story,* p. 61
Her father, Emil Souvestre: Cook, p. 103

59 *Eleanor realized: This Is My Story,* p. 56
"Obviously she had ambition": Anna Roosevelt Halsted, interview by Joseph P. Lash,
   6/22/66, Joseph P. Lash Papers, FDRL
As her friend Isabella: Isabella Ferguson to ER, 12/19/37, ER Papers, FDRL
When Eleanor's cousin: Eleanor and Franklin, p. 84
Corinne Jr., who described: CRA, interview by Hermann Hagedorn, 11/23/54, Her-
   mann Hagedorn Papers, TRCH
Eleanor maintained: ER, "The Seven People Who Shaped My Life," in *Look,* 6/19/51
Corinne Jr. believed: CRA unpublished memoir, copy in possession of Elizabeth
   Winthrop

60 *She became fond: This Is My Story,* pp. 61, 63

New York City's Assembly Ball

Descriptions of the December 1902 New York social season were drawn from newspapers of the day: *NY Herald, NY Tribune, NY Times, NY Evening Journal, Evening
World* (New York), *Mail and Express* (New York), *The Sun* (New York); and the society
magazines *Town Topics* and *Town and Country.*

62 *"What does it matter":* Wharton, *Age of Innocence,* p. 93

63 *One day they decided: Town Topics,* 12/18/02
only Eleanor's name . . . home from parties: ARL diary entries, 12/1902, ARL Papers,
   MDLC

65 *"be the American spirit most":* James, p. 102

65 *ridiculed the pretentiousness:* Mowry, p. 98

"*With my family*": ARL, interview by Hermann Hagedorn, 11/9/54, Hermann Hagedorn Papers, TRCH

Corinne Jr. wished: CRA diary, n.d. 1906, TRCH

66 *She would also wish:* ibid., 1/12/05

She would write that: ER, *Your Teens and Mine,* pp. 47–8

One newspaper pronounced: NY Evening Journal, 12/13/02

"*bright, attractive girls*": Mail and Express, 12/11/02

"*Eleanorish calm*": HRR to ARC, n.d., TRCH

a dowager recalled: Elizabeth Drewry, interview by Dr. Thomas F. Soapes, 9/27/78, ER Oral History Project, FDRL

Eleanor remembered: Your Teens and Mine, p. 48

67 "*As soon as he saw me*": ibid., p. 47

Harris remembered: Lash, *Eleanor and Franklin,* p. 94

Alice would describe: Teague, p. 155

Ferguson came to Eleanor's: Eleanor and Franklin, p. 124

A newspaper remarked: Mail and Express, 12/12/02

"*a great old time*" . . . "*my love and my life*": ARL diary entries for 12/1902–1/1903, ARL Papers, MDLC

68 *Eleanor knew: Your Teens and Mine,* p. 25

An old classmate: Helen Cutting Wilmerding, interview by Joseph P. Lash, 4/29/66, Joseph P. Lash Papers, FDRL

The cousins' aunt Corinne: CRR to CRA, n.d., TRCH

They lunched at . . . morning of shopping: ARL diary entries, 12/1902, ARL Papers, MDLC

in an undated entry: ibid., n.d.

PART TWO

THRESHOLDS

1902–1906

White House New Year

71 *On December 31:* ARL diary, 12/31/02, ARL Papers, MDLC

Franklin had tea: FDR journal, 12/31/02, Roosevelt Family Papers, Business and Personal, FDRL

"*Only a yahoo*": Morison vol. 4, p. 753

His daughter's was: The World (New York), 12/13/02

72 "*a nasty place*": Wister, p. 87

on a trip to Florida: Edith Roosevelt to Ethel Roosevelt Derby, 6/3/[1898], TRCH

Quentin, the youngest: Hagedorn, *Sagamore Hill,* pp. 146–7

chief usher Ike Hoover: Sylvia Jukes Morris, pp. 267–8

swimming in the Potomac: Reminiscences of James Thomas Williams Jr., 1953, vol. 1, p. 154, Columbia U. OH

"*sick and tired*": *Sagamore Hill,* p. 145

Alice thought things: Teague, p. 159

Theodore worried about: Morison, vol. 3, p. 490

The controversial painting: NY Times, 12/14/02

74 *It was a heady experience:* FDR journal, 1/1/03, Roosevelt Family Papers, Business and Personal, FDRL

Boston newspapers: Kleeman, *Gracious Lady,* pp. 226–7

Franklin's example: NY Times, 3/18/02

That fall, his friend: Kleeman, *Young Franklin Roosevelt,* pp. 156–7

When he mentioned: FDR journal, 1/1/03, Roosevelt Family Papers, Business and Personal, FDRL

75 *But suddenly, Eleanor . . . go without them:* ARL diary entries, 1/1/03 and 1/2/03, ARL Papers, MDLC

Another day Eleanor: CRR to CRA, 1/27/03, TRCH

Eleanor claimed later: ER, *This Is My Story,* p. 123

"Eleanor came to see me": CRR to CRA, 4/6 [1903], TRCH

"hardened me": ER, "The Seven People Who Shaped My Life," in *Look,* 6/19/51

she explained that she: Cook, p. 138

"seven deep": Brough, p. 131

"I am an absolute fool": ARL diary, 4/11/03, ARL Papers, MDLC

77 *"No hope for Alice":* ibid., 2/12/02, 3/23/02, 1/3/03

Gherardesca—a "heartless Latin": ibid., 2/1/03, 1/5/03

"John John John": ibid., 6/2/03

Over tea with Edith: ibid., 1/27/03

why he didn't look after her: Wister, p. 87

Corinne was as disturbed: CRR to CRA, 1/3/03, TRCH

78 *When her stepmother:* ARL diary, 1/18/03, ARL Papers, MDLC

First Steps

The details of Alice's trip to Puerto Rico are drawn from the *NY Herald* 3/15/03, 4/6/03; *NY Times* 3/15/03, 3/24/03, 4/1/03, 4/6/03; *NY Tribune* 4/5/03.

79 *Biographers sometimes cite:* Lash, *Eleanor and Franklin,* p. 102; Cook, p. 134; Ward, *Before the Trumpet,* p. 308

In his pocket journal: FDR journal, 12/2/02, 12/9/02, 12/23/02, 1/1/03, 1/30/03, Roosevelt Family Papers, Business and Personal, FDRL

"began coming to": ER, *Your Teens and Mine,* p. 53

"I found myself": ibid., p. 179

At the age of seven: FDR to Elliott Roosevelt, 5/15/89, Roosevelt Family Papers, FDRL

80 *"during the year":* *Your Teens and Mine,* p. 177

"amazed": ibid.

"knew and liked": ibid., p. 176

"Another thing that helped": ibid., p. 178

80 *Eleanor's friends actually thought:* Laura Delano, 6/25 (no year); Margaret Dix Lawrence, 2/18/67; Helen Cutting Wilmerding, 4/29/66, interviews by Joseph P. Lash, Joseph P. Lash Papers, FDRL

On Tuesday afternoons: *Social Register* visiting index 1902

Eleanor later gave: ER, *This Is My Story,* p. 99

81 *Guests often stopped:* *This Is My Story,* p. 101; *Your Teens and Mine,* p. 49

81 *All Eleanor's life: Your Teens and Mine,* p. 107
   Pussie liked to entertain: Margaret Dix Lawrence, interview, 11/14/67, Lash Papers, FDRL
   At Allenswood: Cook, p. 123
   no "dreadful silences": Your Teens and Mine, pp. 53–4
   She was "never uncomfortable": ibid.
   she made her own suggestions: Eleanor and Franklin, p. 126
   Franklin told a friend: Perkins, *The Roosevelt I Knew,* p. 32
   He enjoyed criticizing: Your Teens and Mine, p. 179
   Though they both loved Dickens: ibid., p. 124
   Harvard friends: Lindley, p. 53
   Eleanor liked his "Dutch": This Is My Story, p. 167
   Franklin taught Eleanor: Your Teens and Mine, pp. 123–4
82 *he would proudly advise:* Hickok, p. 111
   Since childhood: Your Teens and Mine, p. 59
   A family retainer: NY Herald Tribune, 7/20/26
   Eleanor treated Hall: Helen Cutting Wilmerding, interview, 4/29/66, Lash Papers, FDRL
   Hall wrote later: Hall Roosevelt, pp. 317–21
   Hall was frightened: This Is My Story, p. 99
84 *"thoroughly good time":* CRR to CRA, 3/12/03, TRCH
   "all the freedom": NY Herald, 3/15/03
   she had carried on: ARL diary 3/22/02 and 4/2/02, ARL Papers, MDLC
85 *"Don't speak of my": NY Times,* 4/6/03
   "Everyone has been so": NY Herald, 4/6/03
   "Darling Alice": Brough, p. 158
   "Oh no one knows": ARL diary, 5/5/03, ARL Papers, MDLC
   Watching her sister: ibid., 7/13/03
   he took Alice to task: Teague, p. 77
86 *"Look at you":* ibid., p. 109
   Early in the summer: ARL diary entries 6/26–7/1/03, ARL Papers, MDLC
   "rather seedy": ibid., 6/29/03
   "about us and": ibid., 6/30/03
   Alice noted in her diary: ibid., 6/27/03
   Several months later: ibid., 12/30/03
   "Oh if only Arthur": ibid., 5/5/03

Vows

The specifics of Theodore's inaugural events come from the *NY Times* 3/4/05 and 3/5/05.

87 *On June 18, 1904: NY Times,* 6/19/04
   "filled with Roosevelts": NY Tribune, 6/19/04
   as "exclusive": ibid.
   The newspapers dwelled: ibid.
88 *In order to arrive in time: NY Times,* 6/19/04
   he had inherited: Pringle, p. 39

He claimed to think: Reminiscences of Marion Dickerman, p. 147, Columbia U. OH

she and her husband had cut: Steeholm, p. 57

Theodore may have mused: TR, *Letters to Kermit,* p. 66

90 *less than a month later:* CRA diary, 7/18/04, TRCH

"I feel very badly for Franklin": CRA, interview by Hermann Hagedorn, 12/28/54, Hermann Hagedorn Papers, TRCH

91 *Alice teased Eleanor:* ARL diary 7/4/04, ARL Papers, MDLC

she would tell: CRA, interview, 12/28/54, Hermann Hagedorn Papers, TRCH

in 1904, she thought: CRA diary, 7/20/04, TRCH

read and discussed: ibid., 7/21/04

At another house party: ibid., 7/31/06

"wanted to live alone": Levy and Russett, p. 33

a "great interest": Lash, *Love, Eleanor,* p. 35

"I entered my": ER, *You Learn by Living,* pp. *103–4*

93 *"very much interested" . . . "like that!":* ER, *Your Teens and Mine,* pp. *180–1*

"cold steel": The World (New York), 7/1/05

he would sign up: Lash, *Eleanor and Franklin,* p. 126

Eleanor wrote Franklin: ibid., p. 134

"either a dreadful flirt": ibid.

he sent a telegram: SDR diary, 7/25/04, Roosevelt Family Papers, FDRL

94 *"I wish you could have seen": Eleanor and Franklin,* p. 135

"Eleanor and Franklin are comic" . . . "both our minds": CRA diary, 10/21/04 and 10/25/04, TRCH

Christine Roosevelt told: Christine Roosevelt to ER, 11/29/04, ER Papers, FDRL

Theodore wrote Franklin: Eleanor and Franklin, p. 138

95 *Corinne Jr. noted:* CRA diary, 11/30/04 and 12/3/04, TRCH

Bye told Eleanor: Ward, *Before the Trumpet,* p. 338

Alice teased Eleanor: Eleanor and Franklin, p. 137

"go on the stump": TR, *Letters to Kermit,* p. 78

Grand Canyon "beautiful": Morison, vol. 3, p. 557

"blank horror": ibid., p. 465

96 *"to be whirled": Letters to Kermit,* p. 59

"church with father": ARL diary, 5/22/04, ARL Papers, MDLC

"church with mother": ibid., 6/12/04

"victoriously, jubilantly": ibid., 11/3/04

"utterly impossible": Letters to Kermit, p. 80

"I am positive": ARL diary, 11/1/04, ARL Papers, MDLC

Theodore declared Parker's charges: NY Tribune, 11/5/04

"I never believe": Letters to Kermit, p. 83

Not until eight years later: Pringle, p. 251

98 *It was part of the image:* Einstein, pp. *8–9*

Eleanor said later: ER, *This Is My Story,* p. 123

James Kearney: Kearney, p. 12

reinforced the dream: Ward, *First Class Temperament,* p. 93

99 *"partly by the glamour": This Is My Story,* p. 166

one biography . . . which Edith: Edith Roosevelt to CRR, 12/14 (no year), TRCH

Lewis Einstein: Einstein, p. 6

his oldest son was known: TR Jr. to Edith Roosevelt, 11/21/05, TR Jr. Papers, MDLC

99 *Theodore told Ted:* TR to TR Jr., 2/6/04, TR Jr. Papers, MDLC
   "in white voile": CRA diary, 3/4/04, TRCH
   "Well, you do it": Teague, p. 72
   "one of the greatest": ibid.

Roosevelt Weds Roosevelt

The particulars of Eleanor's wedding come from the *NY Times* and *The World* (New York), 3/18/05.

101 *As Alice said:* Teague, p. 156
   "Only think of Franklin": Lash, *Eleanor and Franklin,* p. 140
102 *Reporting on her marriage:* The World, 3/18/05
   A few guests complained: Town Topics, 3/23/05
   Alice told an interviewer: Teague, p. 156
   Corinne Jr. wrote: CRA diary, 12/3/04, TRCH
   "more claim to good looks": Town Topics, 3/9/05
   Because Nick had: Eleanor and Franklin, p. 137
104 *Another usher:* ibid.
   "So you are not": Cook, p. 153
   Laura Delano knew: Laura Delano, interview by Joseph P. Lash, 6/25 (no year), Joseph P. Lash Papers, FDRL
   According to friends: Laura Delano, interview, 6/25 (no year); Margaret Dix Lawrence, interview, 2/18/67, Lash Papers, FDRL
   "under her thumb": Laura Delano, interview, 6/25 (no year) Lash Papers, FDRL
   Eleanor had not hesitated: ER, *Your Teens and Mine,* p. 181
   secret code: Ward, *Before the Trumpet,* p. 308
   he once revealed why: ER, "What Is a Wife's Job Today?" in *Good Housekeeping,* 8/1930
   And in a novel: fragment attributed to FDR, n.d., Roosevelt Family Papers, FDRL
   "Franklin calm and happy": SDR diary, 3/17/05, Roosevelt Family Papers, FDRL
105 *"Well, Franklin":* Eleanor and Franklin, p. 141
   "only a fleeting glimpse": Town Topics, 3/23/05
   That night, Alice wrote: ARL diary, 3/17/05, ARL Papers, MDLC
   She had already confessed: ibid., 5/16/03

Alice Rising

106 *"The eyes of the world":* Stacy Rozek Cordery, "Theodore Roosevelt's Private Diplomat: Alice Roosevelt and the 1905 Far Eastern Junket," in Naylor, p. 358
   Russians, whose pogroms: Miller, *Theodore Roosevelt,* p. 443
   During the summer: Cordery, "Theodore Roosevelt's Private Diplomat," in Naylor, p. 355
107 *For months her entries:* ARL diary, 1/29/05–6/17/05, ARL Papers, MDLC
   "Nick and I" . . . "poor little me": ARL diary, 1/19/05, ARL Papers, MDLC
   Theodore instructed Secretary Taft: Pringle, p. 270
   He told newsmen: The World (New York), 7/1/05
108 *one American newspaper began:* ibid., 7/27/05
   "absolutely unprecedented": NY Times, 7/27/05

one Japanese newspaper: Cordery, "Theodore Roosevelt's Private Diplomat," in Naylor, p. 357

"Tired?": Teichmann, p. 42

Half a century later: Teague, p. 87

At a formal dinner: NY Times, 7/27/05

Three days later: Pringle, pp. 269–70

110 *He dodged the delicate:* Abbott, pp. 134–5

Back at the house: Hagedorn, *Sagamore Hill,* pp. 216–17

Despite everything: Pringle, p. 272

"You have established": ibid.

"Everyone is talking": Lash, *Eleanor and Franklin,* p. 150

One day Alice asked: Teichmann, p. 45

111 *Gathering his courage:* Longworth, p. 88

She entertained: Cordery, "Theodore Roosevelt's Private Diplomat," in Naylor, p. 361

hostility toward the United States: Longworth, p. 106

When Alice finally landed: NY Times, 10/24/05

Theodore allowed that: TR, *Letters to Kermit,* p. 120

The reporters wrote: NY Times, 10/27/05

Finally, Alice: Brough, p. 187

Four months later: NY Times, 2/18/06

113 *Even Theodore's "doorkeeper":* ibid.

"by its mere helplessness": Eleanor and Franklin, p. 154

At least one guest: Margaret Cutter, interview by Joseph P. Lash, 8/13/66, Joseph P. Lash Papers, FDRL

two turtle doves: NY Times, 2/18/06

114 *With four possible:* ibid.

"desire for leadership": ibid.

"brisk, kindly Winter": ibid.

115 *but according to her:* Teague, p. 128

Alice later claimed that: ibid.

Theodore stood in the middle: Brough, p. 197

PART THREE

SHIFTING ALLIANCES

1910–1918

Two Cousins Campaign

Franklin's early political career is covered extensively in Geoffrey Ward's *A First Class Temperament.*

119 *"Well," the chairman answered:* Reminiscences of Edward Bernays, 6/5/71, pp. 396–7, Columbia U. OH

"You'll have to": Ward, *First Class Temperament,* p. 108

120 *You fellows":* Hatch, p. 54

one newspaper summed it up: First Class Temperament, p. 112

120 *New York State law:* Roland Redmond, interview by Emily Williams, 10/27/78, ER
Oral History Project, FDRL
121 *at least one journalist:* Gail Sheehy, "Flawless, But Never Quite Loved," NY Times,
6/2/00
"He would approach": Gosnell, p. 29
He had to limp: Rollins, p. 20
121 *Franklin's opponents: First Class Temperament,* p. 120
"anxious to do": Reminiscences of Langdon Marvin, 10/49, p. 69, Columbia U. OH
"there would be": ER, *This Is My Story,* p. 167
worked *"very hard":* Margaret Cutter, interview by Joseph P. Lash, 8/13/66, Joseph P.
Lash Papers, FDRL
123 *NOT TO BE SHOT:* Miller, *Theodore Roosevelt,* p. 510
"The kings": Pringle, p. 368
"late into the night": Longworth, p. 177
They wrote that Franklin: First Class Temperament, p. 130
124 *Theodore had "infected":* ibid., p. 91
"the Crown Prince": ibid., p. 92
Franklin told his friend: ibid., p. 93
He and Teddy Robinson: Lash, *Eleanor and Franklin,* p. 153
Joe Alsop and Corinne Jr.: ibid., pp. 156–7
she made it a rule: Brough, p. 202
125 *"I am more your mother":* James Roosevelt, *My Parents,* p. 25
"in constant competition": Eleanor and Franklin, p. 197
"somewhere between": Miller, *F.D.R.,* p. 70
Terry calculated: Freidel, *The Apprenticeship,* p. 102
"for ten long": F.D.R., p. 74
126 *Franklin thought the group:* Reminiscences of Langdon Marvin, 10/49, p. 46, Columbia U. OH
"led by a": First Class Temperament, p. 134
Eleanor later wrote: This Is My Story, p. 176
one of Franklin's longtime: Reminiscences of Frances Perkins, vol. 1 pt. 2, p. 205,
Columbia U. OH
But behind Franklin's: NY Times, 1/22/11
"During the time": The Apprenticeship, p. 104
Louis Howe had a different: Stiles, p. 33
"an ass of himself": Perkins vol. 1 pt. 2, p. 204, Columbia U. OH
"Just a line to say": F.D.R., p. 75
128 *"That Franklin Roosevelt":* Ross and Grobin, p. 72
Eleanor later claimed: Eleanor and Franklin, p. 173
she got to know them: ibid., p. 172
"political sagacity": ibid., p. 173
"all the sessions" . . . *"approve of this":* Margaret Cutter, interview, 8/13/66, Lash
Papers, FDRL
Langdon Marvin remembered: Langdon Marvin, p. 47, Columbia U. OH
Jennie Delano had: Jennie Delano to Warren Delano, 5/4/06, ER Papers, FDRL
129 *one day destroy: Eleanor and Franklin,* pp. 502, 643
"the only way": ibid., p. 644
"craved to be an individual": This Is My Story, p. 171

he adopted a different: James Roosevelt, *Affectionately, FDR,* p. 44
"*Everyone had a chair*": Grania Gurewitsch, interview by Emily Williams, 9/28/78, ER
    Oral History, FDRL
Usually it took him days: ER, "Churchill at the White House," in *Atlantic,* 3/65
he refused to put one: ER, "Christmas," in *New York American,* 12/24/32
"*They have no*": Pringle, p. 382
130 *had been calling:* Theodore Roosevelt, p. 518
Political observers: Pringle, p. 388
"*The fight is on*": Miller, *Theodore Roosevelt,* p. 522
"*I think she felt*": Brough, p. 216

Divided Loyalties

The account of the Progressive Party Convention is compiled from reports in the *NY
Herald,* 8/5/12–8/8/12; *NY Tribune,* 8/4/12; and *Town and Country,* 8/10/12.

131 "*restless and unhappy*": Lash, *Eleanor and Franklin,* p. 177
Kermit told Franklin: ibid.
"*sticking to their*": *Evening Star* (Washington, D.C.), 6/29/12
132 "*As long as*": *Sunday Evening Star* (Washington, D.C.), 6/30/12
He would launch: Longworth, p. 196
Alice never forgot: ibid., p. 197
133 "*The heir*": *Town Topics,* 5/9/12
Alice and Edith retreated: Longworth, p. 198
young Nicholas Roosevelt: Nicholas Roosevelt, p. 51
The constant roar: Teichmann, p. 87
Archie and Nicholas: Nicholas Roosevelt, p. 53
Alice's uselessness: Longworth, p. 192
134 "*If we are not*": *Eleanor and Franklin,* p. 177
"*appalled*" *when:* ER, *This Is My Story,* p. 188
Eleanor wrote a friend: Cook, p. 197
Rumors swept . . . refused to fly: *Sunday Evening Star,* 6/30/12
spectators wearing Clark buttons: Freidel, *The Apprenticeship,* p. 142
Brisk hand-to-hand: *Sunday Evening Star,* 6/30/12
135 *On Sunday, 100,000 yellow:* Daniels, p. 62
Alice had spent hours: Sylvia Jukes Morris, p. 378
But one afternoon . . . "*frightful disappointment*": Longworth, pp. 211–12
A reporter on the campaign: Abbott, p. 88
137 *Some family members claimed:* Collier with Horowitz, p. 257
even young Nicholas: Nicholas Roosevelt, p. 35
"*liked Franklin very much*": Teague, p. 159
"*I am very anxious*": Cook, p. 214
"*Anything that the*": TR, *Progressive Principles,* p. 220
138 "*plain people*" . . . "*debased and degraded*": ibid., p. 205
"*You may not like*": *Town and Country,* 8/10/12
"*criminal egotism*": *Town Topics,* 8/29/12
"*take the butter*": *NY Herald,* 8/7/12
A rumor went: ibid., 8/6/12

138 *In his address:* Progressive Principles, p. 115
  called for wages: ibid., p. 133
139 *"We stand at":* ibid., p. 173
  If the horizontal beam: NY Herald, 11/3/12
  "The hunt is on": The Apprenticeship, p. 131
  hammering away: Progressive Principles, p. 191
  On the evening of October 14: Nicholas Roosevelt, p. 55
  fifty bullet-riddled pages: Miller, *Theodore Roosevelt*, pp. 530–1
140 *"those little green rooms":* Longworth, p. 218
  Not until Sara: Eleanor and Franklin, p. 178
  "I simply hated": ibid., p. 176
  I can't tell you how: Cook, p. 198
  She spent hours: Longworth, p. 212
  "fomenting such trouble": Brough, p. 224
  But when Alice suggested: Teague, p. 158
  "Everyone says that if": Town Topics, 8/8/12
141 *Edith wished Nick:* Sylvia Jukes Morris, p. 378
  "poor Alice is here": Brough, p. 217
  "It is interesting": Ward, First Class Temperament, p. 200
  "run for Governor": Eleanor and Franklin, p. 188

Wartime Washington

142 *Eleanor sat on the:* Hatch, p. 82
  ever since he had heard: Roland Redmond, interview by Emily Williams, 10/27/78, ER
    Oral History, FDRL
  One said he: Freidel, *The Apprenticeship*, p. 165
143 *She told Franklin that:* Ward, First Class Temperament, p. 186
  "nobody seemed the least": Kilpatrick, p. 8
  "He totally fails": The Apprenticeship, p. 238
144 *He traveled to every:* Hatch, p. 80
  "Some fine day": The Apprenticeship, p. 238
  he wrote a memo: First Class Temperament, p. 301
  Theodore complained: ibid., p. 319
  One evening in March: The Apprenticeship, p. 299
  "vigorous demand about": ibid.
  Some of the cousins: Caroli, p. 408; Cook, p. 223
145 *caught her up on:* Longworth, pp. 263–4
  "We all felt we": CRA unpublished memoir, copy in possession of Elizabeth Winthrop
  "Horrible man": Teague, p. 169
  he told a French gathering: The Apprenticeship, p. 368
  He insisted on: ibid., pp. 358–9n
  Theodore was "very proud": ibid., p. 369n
  Eleanor remembered that: First Class Temperament, p. 346
  the Secret Service: The Apprenticeship, p. 320
146 *Now he enlisted:* Brough, p. 243
  he dropped by: First Class Temperament, p. 344
  Eleanor saw that: ER, *This Is My Story*, p. 250

Franklin told Daniels: First Class Temperament, p. 346

Corinne Jr. later wrote: CRA unpublished memoir, copy in possession of Elizabeth Winthrop

Eleanor was afraid: This Is My Story, p. 230

Like Franklin, she: ibid., p. 250

"Theodore Roosevelt had gone up": The Apprenticeship, p. 302n

"The hats of all": ibid., p. 318

A reporter admiringly: ibid., p. 321

148 *One day she pressed:* Eleanor and Franklin, p. 213

Shocked by the conditions: Schriftgiesser, p. 279

her cousin did: Eleanor and Franklin, p. 192

"always wanted to be": Teague, p. 160

Both young Roosevelts: Levy and Russett, p. 188

149 *she didn't like:* Eleanor and Franklin, p. 215

Colonel Marlborough Churchill: Teague, p. 162

"or something like that": ibid.

"You are a coward": ibid.

Her diary shows: ARL diary, 1/23/10, ARL Papers, MDLC

"I was never": ibid.

In one entry: ibid., 1/6/10

In another: ibid., 2/21/10

Eventually, Alice's name: Felsenthal, pp. 155–7

150 *"looking fairly well":* ER to Isabella Ferguson, 12/27/no year, Greenway Collection, Arizona Historical Society

But though Alice's house: ibid., 6/21/no year

"I always wanted": ARL diary, 1/23/10, ARL Papers, MDLC

"good-looking girls": ARL, interview by Joseph Lash, 2/6/67, Joseph P. Lash Papers, FDRL

because they often: Emily de la Grange, interview, 1/12/67, Lash Papers, FDRL

"family atmosphere" . . . "so maternal": Gladys Saltonstall Brooks, interview, 10/67, Lash Papers, FDRL

"as dear": Carolyn Draper Phillips journal, 2/12/35, ER Papers, FDRL

151 *Much would be made:* Eleanor and Franklin, p. 160

Eleanor thought the two: ER, This I Remember, p. 16

"too much alike": This I Remember, p. 16

It began as a: James Roosevelt, Affectionately, F.D.R., p. 159

Eleanor particularly enjoyed: This Is My Story, p. 197

PART FOUR

SCHISMS

1918–1924

Lucy Mercer

155 *When a congressman:* Brough, p. 278

Teddy Robinson was leading: Anna Roosevelt Halsted, interview by Joseph P. Lash, 11/27/67, Joseph P. Lash Papers, FDRL

155 *It was said:* Lash, *Eleanor and Franklin,* p. 221

156 *Alice said a friend would:* ARL, interview, 4/5/66, Lash Papers, FDRL
She had teased: *Eleanor and Franklin,* p. 226
invited them to dinner: James Roosevelt, *My Parents,* p. 100
been a mere: Teague, p. 158
Alice claimed: ARL, interview, 2/6/67, Lash Papers, FDRL
she wished it could: ibid., 4/5/66
"I really can't stand": *Eleanor and Franklin,* p. 223
One rainy day: ibid.
Not far, Franklin's distant: Alsop, p. 69

157 *"The ways of the group":* ibid., p. 68
"But that": ibid., p. 69
Gladys Saltonstall Brooks: Gladys Saltonstall Brooks, interview, 10/67, Lash Papers, FDRL
The romance was: Aileen Tome, interview, n.d., Lash Papers, FDRL
no "paper trail": Allida M. Black, "For FDR, an Enduring Relationship," in *Washington Post,* 3/1/98
"a really lovely-shaped": Teague, p. 158
Anna Roosevelt believed: Anna Roosevelt Halsted, interview, 11/27/67, Lash Papers, FDRL

158 *a close friend:* Esther Lape, interview, 1/6/70, Lash Papers, FDRL
She said that it was Sara: ARL, interview, 2/6/67, Lash Papers, FDRL
Corinne Jr.'s version: CRA, interview, 4/27 (no year), Lash Papers, FDRL
Franklin and Eleanor's daughter . . . romance suspect: Anna Roosevelt Halsted, interview, 6/22/66, Lash Papers, FDRL

160 *Sara told Eleanor's sister-in-law:* Margaret Cutter, interview, 8/13/66, Lash Papers, FDRL
After "much conferring": ARL, interview, 2/6/67, Lash Papers, FDRL
What is documented: ER, "10 Rules for Success in Marriage," in *Pictorial Review,* vol. 33, 12/1931
Franklin didn't want to hurt: Reminiscences of Anna Roosevelt Halsted, 5/11/73, Columbia U. OH
According to Alice: ARL, interview, 2/6/67, Lash Papers, FDRL
One of Eleanor's: *Eleanor and Franklin,* p. 275

161 *Eleanor might have:* ER to Elinor Morganthau, n.d., ER Papers, FDRL
Corinne Jr. marveled: CRA, interview, 4/27 (no year), Lash Papers, FDRL
A friend, chancing: Alice Draper Carter, interview, 11/21/67, Lash Papers, FDRL
she claimed to be in: *Eleanor and Franklin,* p. 232
"She wasn't disturbed": CRA, interview, 4/16/67, Lash Papers, FDRL
one of their sons: Elliott Roosevelt, interview by Emily Williams, 6/20/79, ER Oral History Project, FDRL
Mrs. Frank Polk: Alsop, p. 72
Later Eleanor mused: Helen Welshimer, "Marriage in the Making," p. 154 (page fragment), FDRL

162 *Looking back, Eleanor:* ER, *It Seems to Me,* p. 34
In the years to come, Eleanor: Lash, *A Friend's Memoir,* p. 196
"absolute self-mastery": ibid.
When years later: Lash, *A Friend's Memoir,* p. 198–9

Peace Treaties

163 *"No one loves two":* ER, *It Seems to Me*, p. 35
"They have all": Sylvia Jukes Morris, p. 413
"green to her grave": ibid., p. 426

165 *It alarmed Theodore:* Miller, *Theodore Roosevelt*, p. 563
Despite his illness: Sylvia Jukes Morris, p. 430
"The old lion": ibid., p. 434
He was buried: ibid., p. 437

166 *The news came:* Ward, *First Class Temperament*, p. 423
Eleanor wrote sadly: Lash, *Eleanor and Franklin*, p. 231
"My eyes," Edith wrote: Edith Roosevelt to CRR, 3/21/19, TRCH
The year before: Brough, p. 250
"Battalion of Death": ibid., p. 255
"It was entirely" . . . "beaten Father": Teague, p. 167

167 *One day several:* Reminiscences of Frances Perkins, vol. 2, pt. 1, p. 69, Columbia U. OH
a delegate came running: Ross and Grobin, pp. 127–8
when the candidates paid: Johnson, pp. 110–11

168 *Franklin alerted people:* Day, p. 55
"Dearest dear Honey": *Eleanor and Franklin*, p. 254
"I can't wait": ibid., p. 252

170 *He had confessed:* ibid., p. 182
"it has been": ibid., p. 255
Someone observed: Perkins, vol. 2, pt. 2, p. 228, Columbia U. OH
and a doctor had: Hagedorn, *Sagamore Hill*, p. 50

171 *A newsman remarked:* undated, unattributed clipping, TR Jr. Papers, MDLC
Bye's son Sheffield: *First Class Temperament*, p. 532
FRANKLIN ROOSEVELT'S CAREER: ibid., p. 531
Eleanor . . . wrote her aunt: Collier with Horowitz, p. 259
"We get asked": *First Class Temperament*, p. 544
William H. Anderson: NY Sun, undated clipping, TR Jr. Papers, MDLC
When Franklin's presidential: Poughkeepsie Courier, undated clipping, TR Jr. Papers, MDLC
Suspicion thickened: Hartley Howe, interview by Joseph P. Lash, 5/5/66, Joseph P. Lash Papers, FDRL

173 *Warren G. Harding:* Collier with Horowitz, p. 259
"that Alice": *Eleanor and Franklin*, p. 254
"He is a maverick": unattributed clipping, 9/7/20, TR Jr. Papers, MDLC
Hall's wife, Margaret: Margaret Cutter, interview, 8/13/66, Lash Papers, FDRL
Alice said later that: Teague, p. 159
on September 24, 1920: Day, p. 61

174 *Not until many years later:* ibid., p. 62
Franklin told a friend: *First Class Temperament*, p. 557

Franklin's Polio

175 *a tour guide points:* Anne Newman, administrative asst. Campobello National Park, interview by the author

176 *The Roosevelts' daughter:* Anna Roosevelt Halsted, interview by Joseph Lash, 6/22/66, Joseph P. Lash Papers, FDRL

Franklin succumbed: Ross and Grobin, p. 133

Just the touch: James Roosevelt, *My Parents*, p. 71–2

As Joseph Alsop: Alsop, p. 95

"Matter of fact": Cook, p. 524

Polio had immobilized: Ward, *First Class Temperament*, p. 586

177 *Years later an interviewer:* ARL, interview, 4/5/66, Lash Papers, FDRL

Sara, arriving back: Lash, *Eleanor and Franklin*, pp. 270–1

but he told one: Gould, p. 29

179 *Years later, Harry:* Reminiscences of Frances Perkins, vol. 7, pt. 4, pp. 556–7 Columbia U. OH

a condition she shared: Teague, p. 112

Owen Wister might: Wister, p. 68

Elliott wrote: Roosevelt and Brough, *Untold Story*, p. 183

180 *James concurred:* James Roosevelt, *Affectionately, F.D.R.*, p.159

One day Nicholas: Nicholas Roosevelt, p. 224

His doctor, George: *Eleanor and Franklin*, p. 272

Louis Howe marveled: Stiles, p. 83

Dynastic Struggle

181 *Once as a child:* Ward, *Before the Trumpet*, p. 145

He invented a traction: Roosevelt and Brough, *Untold Story*, p. 171

Eleanor and Franklin decided: Kearney, p. 101

182 *Eleanor's colleagues remembered:* Marion Dickerman, interview by Joseph P. Lash, 1/30/67, Joseph P. Lash Papers, FDRL

"We are doing": Lash, *Eleanor and Franklin*, p. 279

Franklin met with one: Ward, *First Class Temperament*, p. 675

"crazy": Emma Bugbee, interview, 5/25/70, Lash Papers, FDRL

Franklin had marked off: Collier with Horowitz, p. 294

Now, waiting his turn: James Roosevelt, *My Parents*, p. 93

A friend knew: Reminiscences of Frances Perkins, p. 559, Columbia U. OH

Friends sitting close: ibid.

183 *Alfred E. Smith:* *First Class Temperament*, p. 696

"dry bones rattle": NY Herald Tribune, 6/27/24

"Less blah to": ibid.

Years later, people: Emma Bugbee, interview, 5/25/70, Lash Papers, FDRL

Franklin grasped the lectern: *My Parents*, p. 93

Frances Perkins darted: Perkins, vol. 2, pt. 2, pp. 325–6, Columbia U. OH

"song pluggers": NY Herald Tribune, 6/27/24

One newspaper reported: ibid.

Minutes later: Perkins, vol. 2, pt. 2, p. 327, Columbia U. OH

184 *he had just told:* *First Class Temperament*, p. 684

Would Smith win?: NY Herald Tribune, 6/27/24

"personally nice": ibid.

186 *Frances Perkins noticed:* Perkins, vol. 2, pt. 3, p. 330, Columbia U. OH

Eleanor made it clear: ER, *This I Remember*, p. 31

Later, Eleanor explained: *Eleanor and Franklin,* p. 291

"it was a pretty base": Brough, p. 274

Although Eleanor admitted: *This I Remember,* p. 32

probably the only: John Gable, Executive Director, Theodore Roosevelt Association, interview by the author

Helen Robinson wrote: HRR to ARC, n.d., TRCH

187 *Corinne Jr.'s thirteen-year-old granddaughter:* Elizabeth Winthrop, interview by the author

on election night: CRA unpublished memoir, copy in possession of Elizabeth Winthrop

Whenever they were: TR Jr.'s journal, 1921–23, TR Jr. Papers, MDLC

Her name: CRA unpublished memoir, copy in possession of Elizabeth Winthrop

"If we must have": Brough, p. 290

She relished the stories: Teichmann, p. 117

188 *"Give them the bayonet":* Thomas Curran to TR Jr., 1/14/24, TR Jr. papers, MDLC

"Hit him hard": Anonymous to TR Jr. 9/17/24, TR Jr. Papers, MDLC

They were determined: Odell Hauser, *Providence Journal,* n.d., TR Jr. Papers, MDLC

"I would give": Anonymous to TR Jr., 9/17/24, TR Jr. Papers, MDLC

A reporter claimed: *Brooklyn Times,* n.d., TR Jr. Papers, MDLC

Ted tried on: TR Jr. journal, 9/12/24, TR Jr. Papers, MDLC

"Father's fight": Anna Roosevelt Halsted, interview, 6/22/66, Lash Papers, FDRL

Epilogue

The information on the wartime experiences of both Theodore's and Franklin's sons comes from *The Roosevelts,* by Peter Collier with David Horowitz.

189 *newswoman Lorena Hickok:* Hickok, p. 50

like a gypsy: Edith Roosevelt to TR Jr., n.d., TR Jr. Papers, MDLC

"such poor stuff": Collier with Horowitz, p. 334

On November 8: Miller, *F.D.R.,* p. 289

190 *Nick Longworth had died:* Felsenthal, p. 165

When a reporter: Collier with Horowitz, p. 336

Her blond son: Felsenthal, p. 172

Alice claimed to have: ARL, interview by Joseph P. Lash, 4/5/66, Joseph P. Lash Papers, FDRL

"I really could": Teague, p. 159

One Oyster Bay cousin: CRA, interview by Hermann Hagedorn, 12/28/54, Hermann Hagedorn Papers, TRCH

"Poor little Eleanor": Reminiscences of Frances Perkins, vol. 3, pt. 4, p. 535, Columbia U. OH

191 *"Nobody," Nicholas von Hoffman:* Felsenthal, p. 179

In 1936, in a: Lash, *Eleanor and Franklin,* p. 448

Eleanor, in her syndicated column: ER, *My Day,* vol. 1, p. 34

192 *"entirely of mischief":* Felsenthal, p. 195

"that damned woman": Collier with Horowitz, p. 394

Late one night: Eleanor Wotkyns, interview by Emily Williams, 6/19/78, ER Oral History Project, FDRL

192 *she incurred her husband's:* Eleanor and Franklin, p. 509
193 *Decades later:* Teichmann, pp. 202–3
  and cheered his men: Collier with Horowitz, p. 418
  "emotional homecoming": ibid., p. 399
  When General Omar Bradley: ibid. p. 422
  Ted died in France: ibid., p. 424
195 *"Regardless of the":* ibid., p. 430
  Nicholas . . . recollected: Nicholas Roosevelt, p. 34
  "take my place": ER, *Autobiography,* p. 428
  One day he came: Eleanor and Franklin, p. 390
196 *One of his sons:* ibid., p. 698
  And he had plans: Perkins, p. 762, Columbia U. OH
  When Elliott reported: Roosevelt and Brough, *Untold Story,* pp. 307–8
  Many years later: Suzanne Perrin Kloman, interview by Pat Haas
  Lorena Hickok writes: Streitmatter, p. 54
  Eleanor, in a: ibid., p. 81
  "I never heard": Esther Lape, interview, 2/24/70, Lash Papers, FDRL
  there is a picture: Cook, unpaged photograph
197 *"I could have her":* Untold Story, p. 307
  A double betrayal . . . "again together": Roosevelt and Brough, *Mother R.,* p. 137
  According to the psychiatrist: Dr. Lawrence S. Kubie to ER, 8/22/51, ER Papers, FDRL
198 *"happier with a wife":* ER, *This I Remember,* p. 349
  "was particularly attracted": Levy and Russett, p. 176
  "You must come": ibid.
  "Franklin loved Missy": ibid., p. 175
  Eleanor felt that: This I Remember, p. 349
  "no regrets": ibid.
  Each January 30: Levy and Russett, pp. 177–8
  "The soul that": Goodwin, p. 378
199 *Finding themselves on a train:* Lash, *World of Love,* p. 85
  "if real trouble": Eleanor and Franklin, p. 510
  "vivid & amusing": World of Love, p. 85
  Lawrence Kubie: Dr. Lawrence S. Kubie to ER, 8/22/51, ER Papers, FDRL
  by replying simply: ER to Dr. Lawrence S. Kubie, n.d., ER Papers, FDRL
  She once reprimanded: ARL, interview, 4/5/66, Lash Papers, FDRL
  but sometimes: Collier with Horowitz, p. 475

Abbott, Lawrence F. *Impressions of Theodore Roosevelt.* Garden City, N.Y.: Doubleday, Page & Co., 1919.

Alsop, Joseph. *FDR: A Centenary Remembrance.* New York: Viking Press, 1982.

Amory, Cleveland. *The Last Resorts.* New York: Harper & Bros., 1952.

Bishop, Joseph Bucklin. *Theodore Roosevelt and His Time, Shown in His Letters.* Vols. 1 and 2. New York: Charles Scribner's Sons, 1920.

Brandt, Clare. *An American Aristocracy: The Livingstons.* Garden City, N.Y.: Doubleday & Co., 1986.

Brough, James. *Princess Alice.* Boston: Little, Brown & Co., 1975.

Caroli, Betty Boyd. *The Roosevelt Women.* New York: Basic Books, 1998.

Collier, Peter, with David Horowitz. *The Roosevelts: An American Saga.* New York: Simon & Schuster, 1994.

Cook, Blanche Wiesen. *Eleanor Roosevelt.* Vol. 1 New York: Viking, 1992.

Daniels, Josephus. *The Wilson Era: Years of Peace, 1910–1917.* Chapel Hill, N.C.: University of North Carolina Press, 1944.

Day, Donald, *Franklin D. Roosevelt's Own Story.* Boston: Little, Brown & Co., 1951.

Dows, Olin. *Franklin Roosevelt at Hyde Park.* New York: American Artists Group, 1949.

Einstein, Lewis. *Roosevelt: His Mind in Action.* New York: Houghton Mifflin Co., 1930.

Felsenthal, Carol. *Alice Roosevelt Longworth.* New York: G. P. Putnam's Sons, 1988.

Freidel, Frank. *Franklin D. Roosevelt: The Apprenticeship.* Boston: Little, Brown & Co., 1952.

———. *Franklin D. Roosevelt: A Rendezvous with Destiny.* Boston: Little, Brown & Co., 1990.

Goodwin, Doris Kearns. *No Ordinary Time: Franklin and Eleanor Roosevelt: The Home Front in World War II.* New York: Simon & Schuster, 1994.

Gosnell, Harold Foote. *Champion Campaigner: Franklin D. Roosevelt.* New York: The Macmillan Co., 1952.

Gould, Jean. *A Good Fight: The Story of FDR's Conquest of Polio.* New York: Dodd, Mead & Co., 1960.

Hagedorn, Hermann. *The Roosevelt Family of Sagamore Hill.* New York: The Macmillan Co., 1954.

————. *Roosevelt in the Badlands.* Boston: Houghton Mifflin Co., 1921.

Hatch, Alden. *Franklin D. Roosevelt: An Informal Biography.* New York: Henry Holt & Co., 1947.

Johnson, Gerald W. *Roosevelt: Dictator or Democrat?* New York: Harper & Brothers, 1941.

Kearney, James R. *Anna Eleanor Roosevelt: Evolution of a Reformer.* Boston: Houghton Mifflin, 1968.

Kilpatrick, Carroll, ed. *Roosevelt and Daniels: A Friendship in Politics.* Chapel Hill: University of North Carolina Press, 1952.

Kleeman, Rita Halle. *Gracious Lady: The Life of Sara Delano Roosevelt.* New York: D. Appleton-Century Co. Inc., 1935.

————. *Young Franklin Roosevelt.* New York: Julian Messner, Inc., 1946.

Lash, Joseph P. *Eleanor and Franklin: The Story of Their Relationship, Based on Eleanor Roosevelt's Private Papers.* New York: W. W. Norton & Co., Inc., 1971.

————. *Eleanor Roosevelt: A Friend's Memoir.* Garden City, N.Y.: Doubleday & Co., 1964.

————. *Love, Eleanor: Eleanor Roosevelt and Her Friends.* Garden City, N.Y.: Doubleday & Co., 1982.

————. *A World of Love: Eleanor Roosevelt and Her Friends.* Garden City, N.Y.: Doubleday & Co., 1984.

Levy, William Turner, and Cynthia Eagle Russett. *The Extraordinary Mrs. R: A Friend Remembers Eleanor Roosevelt.* New York: John Wiley & Sons, 1999.

Lindley, Ernest Kidder, *Franklin D. Roosevelt: A Career in Progressive Democracy.* Indianapolis: Bobbs-Merrill Co., 1931.

Longworth, Alice Roosevelt. *Crowded Hours.* New York: Charles Scribner's Sons, 1933.

MacKenzie, Compton. *Mr. Roosevelt.* New York: E. P. Dutton & Co., 1944.

MacLeish, Archibald. *The Eleanor Roosevelt Story.* Boston: Houghton, 1965.

McCullough, David. *Mornings on Horseback.* New York: Simon & Schuster, 1981.

Miller, Nathan. *F.D.R.: An Intimate History.* Garden City, N.Y.: Doubleday & Co., 1983.

————. *Theodore Roosevelt: A Life.* New York: William Morrow & Co., 1992.

Monk, William Everett. *Theodore and Alice: A Love Story.* Interlaken, N.Y.: Empire State Books, 1994.

Morison, Elting E., ed. *The Letters of Theodore Roosevelt.* Vols. 1–8. Cambridge, Mass.: Harvard University Press, 1951–1959.

Morris, Edmund. *The Rise of Theodore Roosevelt.* New York: Coward, McCann & Geoghegan, 1979.

Morris, Sylvia Jukes. *Edith Kermit Roosevelt: Portrait of a First Lady.* New York: Coward, McCann & Geoghegan, 1980.

Mowry, George E. *The Era of Theodore Roosevelt.* New York: Harper & Row, 1958.

Naylor, Natalie, et al., eds. *Theodore Roosevelt: Many-Sided American.* Interlaken, N.Y.: Heart of the Lakes Publishing, 1992.

Perkins, Frances. *The Roosevelt I Knew.* New York: Viking Press, 1946.

Pringle, Henry F. *Theodore Roosevelt: A Biography.* New York: Harcourt Brace & Co., 1956.

Robinson, Corinne Roosevelt. *My Brother Theodore Roosevelt*. New York: Charles Scribner's Sons, 1921.

Rollins, Alfred B., Jr. *Roosevelt and Howe*. New York: Alfred A. Knopf, 1962.

Roosevelt, Eleanor. *The Autobiography of Eleanor Roosevelt*. New York: Harper & Bros., 1958.

———. *Christmas*. New York: St. Martin's Press, 1986.

———. *It Seems to Me*. New York: W. W. Norton & Co., 1954.

———. *My Day*. New York: Pharos Books, 1989.

———. *My Day: The Post-War Years*. Vol. 2. New York: Pharos Books, 1990.

———. *My Day: First Lady of the World*. Vol. 3. New York: Pharos Books, 1991.

———. *This Is My Story*. New York: Harper & Bros., 1937.

———. *This I Remember*. New York: Harper & Bros., 1949.

———. *You Learn by Living*. New York: Harper Bros., 1960.

Roosevelt, Eleanor (with Helen Ferris). *Your Teens and Mine*. Garden City, N.Y.: Doubleday & Co., 1961.

Roosevelt, Elliott. *FDR: His Personal Letters 1905–1928*. New York: Duell, Sloan & Pearce, 1948.

———. *Rendezvous with Destiny*. New York: G. P. Putnam's Sons, 1975.

Roosevelt, Elliott, and James Brough. *Mother R.: Eleanor Roosevelt's Untold Story*. New York: G. P. Putnam's Sons, 1977.

———. *An Untold Story: The Roosevelts of Hyde Park*. New York: G. P. Putnam's Sons, 1973.

Roosevelt, Franklin D. *Complete Press Conferences of Franklin D. Roosevelt*. Vols. 13–14, 1939. New York: DaCapo Press, 1972.

Roosevelt, Hall, in collaboration with Samuel Duff McCoy. *Odyssey of an American Family: An Account of the Roosevelts and Their Kin as Travelers from 1613–1938*. New York: Harper & Bros., 1939.

Roosevelt, James (with Bill Libby). *My Parents: A Differing View*. Chicago: Playboy Press, 1976.

Roosevelt, James, and Sidney Shalett. *Affectionately, F.D.R.: A Son's Story of a Lonely Man*. New York: Harcourt, Brace & Co., 1959.

Roosevelt, Nicholas. *A Front Row Seat*. Norman, Okla.: University of Oklahoma Press, 1953.

Roosevelt, Sara Delano (as told to Isabel Leighton and Gabrielle Forbush). *My Boy Franklin*. New York: Ray Long & Richard R. Smith, 1933.

Roosevelt, Theodore. *Theodore Roosevelt: An Autobiography*. New York: DaCapo Press, 1985.

———, ed. by Elmer H. Youngman. *Progressive Principles: Selections from National Addresses Made During the Presidential Campaign of 1912*. New York: Progressive National Service, 1913.

———. *Letters to Kermit from Theodore Roosevelt 1902–1908*. New York: Charles Scribner's Sons, 1946.

———. *The Works of Theodore Roosevelt: National Edition*. Vol. 1. New York: Charles Scribner's Sons, 1926, 1927.

Roosevelt, Theodore, Jr. *All in the Family*. New York: G. P. Putnam's Sons, 1929.

Ross, Leland M., and Allen W. Grobin. *This Democratic Roosevelt: The Life Story of "F.D."* New York: E. P. Dutton & Co., Inc., 1932.

Schriftgiesser, Karl. *The Amazing Roosevelt Family*. New York: W. Funk, Inc., 1942.

Sewall, William. *Bill Sewall's Story of T.R.* New York: Harper & Bros., 1919.

Social Register. New York, 1902.

Steeholm, Clara, and Hardy Steeholm. *The House at Hyde Park.* New York: Viking Press, 1950.

Stiles, Lela. *The Man Behind Roosevelt: The Story of Louis McHenry Howe.* Cleveland: World Publishing Co., 1954.

Streitmatter, Roger, ed. *Empty Without You: The Intimate Letters of Eleanor Roosevelt and Lorena Hickok.* New York: The Free Press, 1998.

Teague, Michael. *Mrs. L: Conversations with Alice Roosevelt Longworth.* Garden City, N.Y.: Doubleday & Co., 1981.

Teichmann, Howard. *Alice: The Life and Times of Alice Roosevelt.* Englewood Cliffs, N.J.: Prentice-Hall, 1979.

Tugwell, Rexford. *The Democratic Roosevelt: A Biography of Franklin D. Roosevelt.* Garden City, N.Y.: Doubleday & Co., 1957.

Ward, Geoffrey C. *Before the Trumpet: Young Franklin Roosevelt 1882–1905.* New York: Harper & Row, 1985.

———. *A First Class Temperament: The Emergence of Franklin Roosevelt.* New York: Harper & Row, 1989.

Wharton, Edith. *The Age of Innocence.* New York: Simon & Schuster, 1996.

Wister, Owen. *Roosevelt: The Story of a Friendship.* New York: The Macmillan Co., 1930.

Wolfe, Gerard. *New York: A Guide to the Metropolis: Walking Tours of Architecture and History.* New York: McGraw-Hill, 1983.

Collections

Columbia University Oral History Research Office Collection, New York City, New York

Greenway Collection, Arizona Historical Society, Tucson, Arizona

Theodore Roosevelt Collection, Harvard College Library, by permission of the Houghton Library, Harvard University, Cambridge, Massachusetts

The Carlton Putnam Papers
The Hermann Hagedorn Papers
The Endicott Peabody Papers

Manuscript Division at the Library of Congress, Washington, D.C.

Theodore Roosevelt Papers
Theodore Roosevelt Jr. Papers
Alice Roosevelt Longworth Papers

Franklin D. Roosevelt Research Library, Hyde Park, New York

Joseph P. Lash Papers
Eleanor Roosevelt Oral History Project
Eleanor Roosevelt Papers
Roosevelt Family Papers
Roosevelt Family Papers, Donated by Children
Roosevelt Family Papers, Business and Personal

A C K N O W L E D G M E N T S

I am grateful to my friend Elizabeth Winthrop, whose suggestion that I write a book about three Roosevelt first cousins—her grandmother Corinne Robinson, Eleanor Roosevelt, and Alice Roosevelt—prompted this project. As a Roosevelt, Elizabeth was an invaluable guide through the family lore, and, fine novelist that she is, a writing companion of the most generous order.

Much of the research for this book took place in the Franklin D. Roosevelt Library in Hyde Park, New York; the Rare Book and Manuscript Division of the Library of Congress in Washington, D.C.; and the Manuscript Room of Harvard University's Houghton Library in Cambridge, Massachusetts. Without exception, everyone whose help I sought was kind, and while there is not space to list each person by name, I would like to note that this book could not have been accomplished without them.

Wallace Dailey, in charge of the Theodore Roosevelt Collection at Harvard, was thorough and patient in dealing with my many research questions over the course of several years, and he led me to material I would have been slow to find otherwise or would not have found at all. In Oyster Bay, New York, over many conversations, the head of the Theodore Roosevelt Association, Dr. John A. Gable, shared his encyclopedic knowledge of the Roosevelt family, as well as his perceptions of their various relationships. I thank him for his careful attention to the manuscript and for his suggestions at several junctures. The fact that book writing takes time gives strangers a chance to become friends, and, from my standpoint, at least, that alchemy was achieved with Wallace and John.

Making books can challenge relationships as well as create them, because the writer may be incapable of talking about anything else for years on end. I appreciate the patience of my friends. Lucy Borge, Tom Crider, Connie Fulenwider, Elizabeth Hunnewell, Steve Kellogg, Reeve Lindbergh, Montie Mills, Annie Rohrmeier, and Ellen Warner read the text at different stages, and their comments informed later drafts. I admire their editorial acuity as much as I admire their good temper.

As important were the practical contributions of other friends. My thanks to Janet Foster, who managed to coordinate the notes and to fact-check while keeping a weather eye on a constantly changing text. Judy Wilson spent time with the manuscript, then turned to the details of the photo research, in this case an extensive task. These longtime friends were a pleasure to work with at all moments.

My agent, Julian Bach, began this project with me but is now retired. He has been a friend for many years, and I miss his wise counsel, but I appreciate the support of his colleague Carolyn Krupp at IMG/Literary. My thanks to my editor, Pat Hass, who shared my enthusiasm from the first and gave me the opportunity to publish this book, and my appreciation to Nancy Nicholas for stepping in at moments to subdue the text, and to Joanna Sturm for allowing me to quote from her grandmother Alice Roosevelt Longworth's diary. My thanks, too, to Dr. John F. Sears, who generously contributed research helpful to this project, and who kindly reviewed the final draft. But no one, however well-intended, can save a writer from all of his or her mistakes. The caveat—that missteps belong to the author—is familiar because it is true.

With luck, a solitary endeavor needn't be lonely. My father, ninety-one years old, has been interested in the Roosevelt cousins since I began my research. My husband, Tony, was where I turned when I needed support and where I found it— and this has been true for more years than it took to write this book. Throughout, I was particularly sustained by the fellow feeling with which our children, Cassin, Alexander, and Michael, continued to greet cousins not their own. It is not for form's sake that their names are found along with their father's both at the beginning of the book, in the dedication, and here, at the end.

Page numbers in *italics* refer to illustrations. TR refers to Theodore Roosevelt,
ER to Eleanor Roosevelt, FDR to Franklin Delano Roosevelt,
and ARL to Alice Roosevelt Longworth.

The illustrations in this book are used by permission and courtesy of the following:

© Bettmann/CORBIS: pp. 5 (left), 43 (right), 46 (bottom left), 64 (top right), 178 (bottom)

© CORBIS: pp. 73 (bottom), 194 (bottom right)

FDR Library: pp. 5 (right), 8 (top left), 26 (right), 31, 34 (top, bottom left), 39 (right top, bottom), 54, 58 (top left, bottom), 64 (top left, bottom), 83 (top, middle), 89 (bottom left and right), 92, 97 (top left), 103, 122 (bottom), 127 (top right, bottom left), 159, 169 (middle, bottom), 172 (top left), 178 (middle), 185 (top left, bottom left), 194 (top right, bottom left)

Theodore Roosevelt Collection, Harvard College Library: pp. 8 (right, bottom), 15 (top left), 16 (top), 20, 23 (bottom), 26 (bottom), 39 (left), 43 (left, bottom), 46 (top, bottom right), 58 (top right), 73 (top, middle), 76, 83 (bottom), 89 (top), 97 (top right, middle, bottom), 109, 112, 122 (top left and right), 136, 147 (top left, right, middle), 164, 169 (top), 172 (top right, bottom), 178 (top), 185 (bottom right), 194 (top left)

Theodore Roosevelt Collection, Harvard College Library. By permission of the Houghton Library, Harvard University: pp. 15 (right, bottom left), 23 (right top), 58 (middle right).

Theodore Roosevelt Collection, Harvard College Library. By permission of the Houghton Library, Harvard University and Elizabeth Winthrop: pp. 16 (bottom), 23 (left), 26 (left), 127 (top left), 147 (bottom)

© Underwood & Underwood/CORBIS: pp. 34 (bottom right), 127 (bottom right), 185 (top right)

A NOTE ABOUT THE AUTHOR

Linda Donn is the author of *Freud and Jung: Years of Friendship, Years of Loss* and holds an M.A. in clinical psychology from the New School for Social Research. She and her husband have three children and divide their time between New York City and Vermont.

A   NOTE   ON   THE   TYPE

This book was set in Fairfield Light, the first typeface from the hand of the distin-guished American artist and engraver Rudolph Ruzicka (1883–1978). In its structure Fairfield displays the sober and sane qualities of the master craftsman whose talent has long been dedicated to clarity. It is this trait that accounts for the trim grace and vigor, the spirited design and sensitive balance, of this original typeface.

Rudolph Ruzicka was born in Bohemia and came to America in 1894. He set up his own shop, devoted to wood engraving and printing, in New York in 1913 after a varied career working as a wood engraver, in photoengraving and banknote printing plants, and as an art director and freelance artist. He designed and illustrated many books, and was the creator of a considerable list of individual prints—wood engravings, line engravings on copper, and aquatints.

Composed by North Market Street Graphics, Lancaster, Pennsylvania
Printed and bound by Quebecor Printing, Fairfield, Pennsylvania
Designed by Ralph Fowler